A Practical Guide to Problem-based Learning Online

'Maggi has a real knack for exploring the pragmatic with a critical eye. The "how to" of PBL online is tempered by a "why should", while tantalizing us with the "what could be". This is a book with some big ideas that compel us to envision PBL "futures"'.
Glen O'Grady, Director, Centre for Educational Development, Republic Polytechnic, Singapore

'A skilful blend of practical wisdom and scholarly insight. This book succeeds in the difficult task of both encouraging newcomers and providing thought-provoking material for old hands'.
Della Freeth, Professor of Professional and Interprofessional Education, City University, London

A Practical Guide to Problem-based Learning Online provides highly grounded research-based guidance for educators wanting to change from face-to-face problem-based learning to online approaches. Offering a comprehensive overview of the current status of problem-based learning online, Maggi Savin-Baden outlines common mistakes and assumptions to avoid future problems and shows how to facilitate learning effectively. It is a text that examines existing forms of provision and suggests the reasons for the increasing popularity of online approaches. Including resources for games and activities, problem-based learning scenarios in different disciplines, advice for supporting staff and students, along with evaluations of software and curriculum designs needed for learning, *A Practical Guide to Problem-based Learning Online* is an essential text for all educators involved in the design and delivery of problem-based learning online.

Maggi Savin-Baden is Professor of Higher Education Research and Director of the Learning Innovation Group at Coventry University, UK.

A Practical Guide to Problem-based Learning Online

Maggi Savin-Baden

Routledge
Taylor & Francis Group

LONDON AND NEW YORK

First published 2007
by Routledge
270 Madison Ave, New York, NY 10016

Simultaneously published in the UK
by Routledge
2 Park Square, Milton Park, Abingdon, Oxon OX14 4RN

Routledge is an imprint of the Taylor & Francis Group, an informa business

Typeset in Times New Roman and Gill Sans by
Florence Production Ltd, Stoodleigh, Devon
Printed and bound in Great Britain by
TJ International Ltd, Padstow Cornwall

Library of Congress Cataloging in Publication Data
Savin-Baden, Maggi, 1960–
  A practical guide to problem-based learning online/
Maggi Savin-Baden.
        p. cm.
    Includes bibliographical references and index.
  1. Problem-based learning.   2. Computer-assisted instruction.
  I. Title.
LB1027.42.S278 2008
371.33′4 – dc22   2007024806

British Library Cataloguing in Publication Data
A catalogue record for this book is available from the British Library

ISBN10: 0–415–43787–3 (hbk)
ISBN10: 0–415–43788–1 (pbk)
ISBN10: 0–203–93814–3 (ebk)

ISBN13: 978–0–415–43787–5 (hbk)
ISBN13: 978–0–415–43788–2 (pbk)
ISBN13: 978–0–203–93814–0 (ebk)

For Anna

Contents

Illustrations

Figures

Tables

Boxes

Acknowledgements

Thanks are due to Madeline Atkins, a rare vice chancellor, who allowed me to take risks and try things out (pedagogically, of course). Thanks are also due to Sheila Leddington Wright for realigning my back when it and I spent too much time huddled over a computer – as well as the critical conversations during the physiotherapy. Thanks are also due to Gilly Salmon for encouraging me to take on this project and providing critical comments on the proposal.

I am also grateful to all those who allowed me to use their materials and offered honest comments, they are: Sian Bayne, Chris Beaumont, Chew Swee Cheng, Maija Kärnä, Petra Luck, Hamish Macleod, Geoff Norton, Sari Poikela, Frans Ronteltap, Christine Sinclair, Rhona Sharpe, Terry Stewart, Pirjo Vuoskoski, Kay Wilkie and Wilco te Winkel.

My immense thanks are also due to John Savin-Baden for his support, critique and proofreading.

The views expressed here and any errors are mine.

Abbreviations

CBIT	Centre for Biological Information Technology
CEO	Chief Executive Officer
CIPP	Context, Inputs, Process, Products
CMC	Computer mediated communication
EPR	Electronic Patient Records
EUR	Erasmus University Rotterdam
FRAP	Form for the Reading of the Analysis of Problems
ICT	Information and Communications Technology
ISDN	Integrated Services Digital Network
ISP	Internet Service Provider
MLE	Managed learning environment
MSN	Microsoft Network
MUVEs	Multi-User Virtual Environments
PBL	Problem-based Learning
PBLi	PBL-interactive
PBLonline	Problem-based Learning online
POLARIS	Problem Oriented Learning and Retrieval Information System
SEM	Sport and Exercise Medicine
SL/PBL	Second Life/Problem-based Learning
SLURL	Second Life Uniform Resource Locator
SONIC	Students Online in Nursing Integrated Curricula
TPLD	Team Play Learning Dynamics
UM	Maastricht University
VLE	Virtual learning environment
WAN	Wide area network

Introduction
Problem-based learning in context

Introduction

The purpose of this book is to provide highly grounded research-based ways for those wanting to change problem-based learning modules and programmes from face-to-face to online approaches. It will also be useful for those who have developed e-learning components and who want to adopt problem-based methods. Using electronic means to deploy problem-based learning within higher education is an area needing more support in all disciplinary areas, but particularly in health, medicine, education and social care, since these are already advanced non-online users of problem-based learning in higher education.

This introduction sets the scene for the book as a whole by providing some illustrative examples of the kinds of issues and concerns that are coming to the fore in this field from the perspectives of staff involved in designing and implementing problem-based learning online.

Problem-based learning

The notion of learning through managing problems is not new, and the emergence and development of problem-based learning reflects a number of historic changes in understandings of learning and the shaping of higher education worldwide. For example, in the 1960s educators began to question traditional teaching methods where the staff member acted as the primary vehicle of information. The negotiation of meaning, the focus on experience and the development of sound social practices and ideologies began to be viewed as central to the exploration of the nature of knowledge. As these ideas converged with other contextual forces, space opened for change, and problem-based learning emerged as an innovative approach to education.

Although there are several blueprints for problem-based learning, relatively little information exists to guide those who want to consider how to use it in terms of actually designing the curriculum in a practical way. Cultural and institutional constraints affect the design of problem-based curricula, as do issues that tend to differ across disciplines, such as the way an essay is constructed or the way that knowledge is seen. Thus, early definitions of problem-based learning identify the classic model as one that has the following characteristics (Barrows and Tamblyn, 1980):

- Complex, real world situations that have no one 'right' answer are the organizing focus for learning.
- Students work in teams to confront the problem, to identify learning gaps, and to develop viable solutions.
- Students gain new information though self-directed learning.
- Staff act as facilitators.
- Problems lead to the development of clinical problem-solving capabilities.

The book begins in Chapter 1 by examining the many reasons why problem-based learning is being moved away from a face-to-face mode of learning to a virtual form. It will present the relevant literature and examine the extent to which the pedagogies associated with both approaches complement each other or collide. The second chapter explores the challenges of using problem-based learning and forms of online learning together and it will examine the relation between them. This chapter explains the particular types on offer and illustrates these with examples from around the world. In particular, it will analyse the differing formulations of problem-based learning online that are available and critique the advantages and disadvantages of the various approaches. Many in the field of problem-based learning have felt that it could be easily adapted to online environments, but have found this more difficult than they had envisaged and this is explored in Chapter 3. This chapter will examine the mistakes others have made and suggest alternative strategies. Chapter 3 will also include reflections from experts in the field regarding their design decisions; choices and views about what they would do were they were attempting it again for the first time. The final section in Part 1, Chapter 4 debunks some of the myths about facilitating PBLonline, and in particular the idea that has been seen by some as an easier (or more difficult) option than managing face-to-face facilitation. It will argue that different approaches to facilitation are needed depending on the form of PBLonline adopted.

Part 2 of this book focuses on issues of design and implementation of problem-based learning in online environments. It begins with Chapter 5, which raises questions for the reader relating to design choices regarding e-problem-based learning and offers the reader ways of making informed design decisions. It begins by exploring some of the issues that need to be considered when designing PBLonline, not from a technological perspective but from a pedagogical one. By starting with what it is we want students to learn it is argued that we can focus on the students' experience rather than the notion of content coverage. It is important too to move away from the idea of PBLonline being a course that uses knowledge repository. Instead this chapter will suggest, by using a design scheme that focuses on learning intentions, assessment and the development of capability, that the kinds of PBLonline on offer will concentrate on liquid learning and the ability of students to develop judgments, criticality and the ability to interrogate texts. Chapter 6 will explore the choices and decisions that need to be made when deciding which form of PBLonline to adopt. It will examine examples from around the world, in order to exemplify how different forms can work well, merely survive or fail. It will raise questions for the reader relating to design choices regarding PBLonline learning and offer the reader ways of making informed design decisions through the use of a series of steps. It will also explore the complexities of managing effective online collaboration and group dynamics and use mini case studies to illustrate success and failure from those experienced in this field. The final chapter, Chapter 7, explores the future possibilities for using PBLonline; particular in the context of social software characterized through the Web 2.0 and Web 3.0 movements. It explores the likely impact of wikis, blogs and learning in 3D virtual worlds on the PBL community, and offers suggestions and exemplars about how PBL might be used differently in the future. This chapter seeks to present a challenge to the problem-based learning community about the possibilities for reinventing problem-based learning as both a philosophy and an approach to learning.

The final section of the book, Part 3, offers a series of resources to support the design and implementation of problem-based learning online. The section on 'Building online teams' will suggest a series of games and activities that help to build not only online teams but also online problem-based learning teams. Building teams in face-to-face problem-based settings is an area that has gained increasing attention in the problem-based learning community. However, it has been recognized that building online teams requires considerably more effort than for face-to-face teams, in order to ensure that the problem-based teams work effectively together (for example, Savin-Baden and Wilkie, 2006). 'Scenarios that work' is a section that considers the nature of problem scenarios in problem-based learning online. The issue of what might count as a problem and the complexity of problem design is something that is a challenge to many tutors implementing problem-based learning, whether face-to-face or in online contexts. Some people design the problems themselves; others use templates or download problems that can be adapted. This section will illustrate a number of scenarios that work well online and will demonstrate the way in which links and supporting material are used to enhance team collaboration. 'Assessing PBLonline' offers suggestions about how best to design and implement assessment. Many of the issues regarding assessment require no less thought and care than they need under other approaches to learning and teaching. However, there are many examples of where assessment has been out of alignment with other aspects of the curriculum. This section presents principles of assessment and explores ways in which assessment may be undertaken in ways that support the shift to Web 2.0 technologies. 'E-valuating PBLonline' will suggest ways of undertaking evaluations of problem-based learning online. It will suggest that evaluation needs to explore problem-based learning online from a number of perspectives, including technical perspectives, organizational perspectives and pedagogical perspectives. It will also suggest which forms of evaluation fit best with problem-based learning online.

This text is designed to be practical and offer insights from those with experience of implementing PBLonline in various ways in a number of disciplines. It is not designed to be a comprehensive guide through the design and implementation of PBLonline, although a number of pointers are given; rather it offers suggestions and perspectives that to date have been underexplored and offers some possibilities for rethinking PBLonline for the future.

Part I

Deciding how to implement problem-based learning online

Chapter 1

Reasons for implementing problem-based learning online

Introduction

This chapter will examine the reasons why problem-based learning is being moved from a face-to-face mode of learning to a virtual form. It will present the relevant literature and examine the extent to which the pedagogies associated with both approaches complement each other or collide. It begins by presenting a few of the current face-to-face approaches available and suggesting ways of beginning to design a PBLonline module. It then explores the reasons why there is an increasing use of PBLonline and suggests issues that need to be considered in relation to implementation.

Although problem-based learning has been used for many years and in diverse ways, the use of it as an online teaching approach is relatively new. The reasons for using PBLonline are many and various, yet most people who have developed PBLonline have begun by using it face-to-face in the first instance. While it is possible to set up PBLonline from scratch, I would suggest that having some face-to-face experience beforehand is useful. This is because facilitating problem-based learning teams is markedly different from other forms of teaching and certainly differs significantly from the general types of moderation used in online environments. However, discussion about the relationship between facilitation and moderation is undertaken fully in Chapter 4.

Overview of problem-based learning

In the last decade problem-based learning has changed considerably. For a once relatively stable and clear approach to teaching, with a number of models and variations, which shared similar philosophies and perspectives, the current landscape is diverse, complex and contested. The result of such diversity is a landscape of both confusion and enthusiasm, which has resulted in overlapping concepts, terms, ideas and views about what once counted as problem-based learning. This first part of the chapter part begins by presenting some of the early models and approaches, but mainly focuses on the ones still in use today. The second section of this chapter explores more recent formulations of problem-based learning and discusses the relationship between problem-based learning and types of inquiry-based learning.

Problem-based learning was an approach popularized by Barrows and Tamblyn (1980) following their research into the reasoning abilities of medical students at McMaster Medical School in Canada. This was because they found that students could learn content and skill, but when faced with a patient could not apply their knowledge in the practical situation. Barrows and Tamblyn's study and the approach adopted at McMaster marked a clear move away from problem-solving learning in which individual students answered a series of questions from information supplied by a lecturer. Rather, this new method they proposed involved learning in ways that used problem scenarios to encourage students to engage themselves in the learning process, a method that became known as problem-based learning. In this early version of problem-based learning certain key characteristics were essential (Box 1.1). Students in small teams[1] would explore a problem situation and through this exploration were expected to examine the gaps in their own knowledge and skills in order to decide what information they needed to acquire in order to resolve or manage the situation with which they were presented. Thus, early definitions of problem-based learning identify the classic model as one that has the characteristics shown in Box 1.1 (Barrows and Tamblyn, 1980).

Soon after McMaster began its problem-based learning curriculum two other new medical schools, at the University of Limburg at Maastricht in the Netherlands and at the University of Newcastle in Australia, adapted the McMaster model of problem-based learning and in so doing developed their own spheres of influence. The then University of Limburg, now Maastricht, began a new medical school in 1975, which saw problem-based learning as the primary strategy for the first four study years. The institution developed a new library consistent with the problem-based learning approach in 1992 (Ebenezer, 1993). The seven steps developed by them are still used in

---

Box 1.1 Characteristics of problem-based learning

- Complex, real world situations that have no one 'right' answer are the organizing focus for learning.
- Students work in teams to confront the problem, to identify learning gaps, and to develop viable solutions.
- Students gain new information though self-directed learning.
- Staff act as facilitators.
- Problems lead to the development of clinical problem-solving capabilities.

Box 1.2 Maastricht seven steps to problem-based learning

1 Clarify and agree working definitions, unclear terms and concepts.
2 Define the problem and agree which phenomena require explanation.
3 Analyse the problems (brainstorm).
4 Arrange explanations into a tentative solution.
5 Generate and prioritize learning objectives.
6 Research the objectives through private study.
7 Report back, synthesize explanations and apply new information to the original problems.

---

curricula worldwide, although more often in subjects such as medicine, psychology and health sciences rather than arts-based subjects (Box 1.2).

Problem-based learning also became popular in Australia, perhaps spurred on in part by the Karmel Report in 1973 that concluded that Australian medical school curricula were too science-oriented (Report on the Committee for Medical Schools, 1973).

There are a number of leading debates in the field of problem-based learning. One of these related to the extent to which a course, module or programme is deemed to be problem-based or not. To date there has been little in-depth discussion about the design of problem-based curricula. Instead the discussions have tended to centre on what counts as problem-based learning, ways of implementing it and types of problem-based learning (for example, Boud, 1985; Barrows, 1986). More recently Conway and Little (2000) have suggested that problem-based learning tends to be utilized as either an instructional strategy or as a curriculum design. Instructional strategy is where problem-based learning is largely seen as another teaching approach that can be mixed in with other approaches. Thus, it tends to be used within a subject or as a component of a programme or module, where other subjects may be delivered through lectures. In an integrated problem-based learning curriculum, there is a sense of problem-based learning being a philosophy of curriculum design that promotes an integrated approach to both curriculum design and learning. Here, students encounter one problem at a time and each problem drives the learning. A number of other discussions have emerged about types of problem-based learning, the most basic being that there are two types: the pure model and the hybrid model. The argument here is that either the whole curriculum is problem-based and is modelled on the McMaster version of problem-based learning, whereby students meet in small teams and do not receive lectures or tutorials, or it is the hybrid model, which is usually defined by the inclusion of fixed resource sessions such as lectures and tutorials which are designed to support students. Lectures may be timetabled in advance or may be requested by the students at various points in the module or programme. The so-called pure model is also often termed the Medical School Model, and is invariably defined as necessarily having a dedicated facilitator for small teams of students, being student centred and being seen to be a good choice for highly motivated, experienced learners in small cohorts (see for example, Duch *et al.*, 2001). The difficulty with this notion of there only being two types: a pure model and a hybrid model, is that in reality given the current number of forms of problem-based learning in existence, most models would be classed as being hybrid. I would therefore suggest that:

> Problem-based learning is thus an approach to learning that is characterized by flexibility and diversity in the sense that it can be implemented in a variety of ways in and across different subjects and disciplines in diverse contexts. As such it can therefore look very different to different people at different moments in time depending on the staff and students involved in the programmes utilizing it. However, what will be similar will be the focus of learning around problem scenarios rather than discrete subjects.
>
> (Savin-Baden, 2000: 3)

One of the other main debates centres around the relationship between problem-based learning and other forms of learning. It is possible, in many conventional curricula, to add on project-based learning, games, simulations and work-based learning in a whole variety of ways. However, bolting on problem-based learning is usually quite difficult because of the need for inquiry and student-centred practices to be central to the whole learning approach.

The values implicit in problem-based learning

One of the central issues about problem-based learning as an approach is the values upon which is based. These values centre on education as the practice of freedom and the ideals that students (and staff) need to 'transgress those boundaries that would confine each pupil to a rote, assembly-line approach to learning' (hooks, 1994: 13). For example, those from the field of adult and community education would argue that this position is one to strive for, and indeed Mezirow has argued for a critical theory of adult learning in which our 'meaning perspectives' guide our understanding of our relationships and ourselves, and are transformed through reflection on the grounds of our beliefs (Mezirow, 1981, 1991). Mezirow's theories and models are based on the assumption that we each have constructions of reality which are dependent upon reinforcement from various sources in the socio-cultural world. These constructions of reality, our 'perspectives', are transformed when an individual's perspective is not in harmony with their experience. In the situation of perspective transformation the individual's construction of reality is transformed as a result of reflecting upon the experience, and plotting new strategies of living as a result of his assessment of the situation.

Freire (1974) adopted a more political stance by exploring how deeply embedded values affect dialogue. The socio-cultural background from which Freire's theory emerged, the oppression of the masses in Brazil by an elite who reflected the dominant values of a non-Brazilian culture, resulted in him depicting the objectified culture as being false and hostile to the culture of the indigenous learner. The crux of Freire's argument is that no education can be neutral since the culture of the oppressed is in opposition to that of the elite. Freire (1974) adopted the term 'conscientization' to describe the process whereby people come to understand that their view of the world and their place in it is shaped by social and historical forces that work against their own interests. He argued that the oppressed lack a critical understanding of their reality, thus the emphasis in learning from a Freirian perspective is on the dialogue between the teacher-learner and the learner-teacher. Freire regards the teacher as a facilitator who is able to stimulate the learning process (rather than one who teaches 'correct' knowledge and values). However, although Freire dealt with issues of power and oppression, much of his work is largely disregarded, or unknown in most disciplines in higher education.

Problem-based learning in different disciplines

In addition to influencing medical education worldwide, McMaster, Maastricht and Newcastle had considerable influence upon each other as well. According to Barrows (2000), many of the educators at Maastricht and Newcastle spent considerable time at McMaster while working to develop their new curricula. Fertilization and cross-pollination of ideas allowed the model to grow and also kept the three universities fairly congruent in their approaches. However, there have also been differences in the way in which problem-based learning has been adopted in different disciplines within other institutions. For example, other health-related programmes began to use problem-based learning from the 1980s onwards. These included programmes such as veterinary medicine at Mississippi State University, USA, pharmacy at Samford University, USA, and nursing at the universities of North Carolina, USA, and Newcastle, Australia. In the UK during the 1980s problem-based learning was adopted in occupational therapy at the then West London Institute of Higher Education and The London Hospital Medical School, and in social work education at the University of Bristol.

Problem-based learning soon began to move beyond its origins to other professional preparation programmes such as engineering at McMaster and Coventry University and Imperial College, London in the UK; business at Maastricht University, The Netherlands and education at Stanford University, USA (Casey and Howson, 1993; Bridges and Hallinger, 1996; Major, 1999). Other disciplines in which problem-based learning is used around the world include architecture, economics, educational administration, law, forestry, optometry, police science and social work (Cordeiro and Campbell, 1996; Bridges and Hallinger, 1996; Boud and Feletti, 1997). Problem-based learning in education for the professions has also been adopted at universities in Denmark, Finland, France, South Africa and Sweden, to name but a few.

How problem-based learning is used: a basic overview

Although problem-based learning is used differently by different people in diverse disciplines and contexts, a useful starting point is to consider implementation in the following way. This is a building block approach through which the curriculum design can be adapted and changed to suit the discipline, and the length and type of the scenarios can also be modified. The 'problems', also termed 'scenarios' are central to student learning in each component of the curriculum (modules/units), as in Figure 1.1. The lectures, seminars, workshops or laboratories support the inquiry process rather than transmitting subject-based knowledge. Whether it is a module or a whole programme that is being designed, the starting point should be a set of problem scenarios that enable students to become independent inquirers and help them to see learning and knowledge as flexible entities.

The curriculum is located around 'scenarios' set within an explicit educational philosophy and designed with problem scenarios central to student learning and to each component of the curriculum. Teaching and assessment methods support and inform student inquiry.

Perhaps one of the easiest ways to begin is to think of designing a 12-week block, as illustrated in Figure 1.2. Here a problem scenario extends over 3 weeks, with a 2-hour seminar per week plus support resources, according to the relevant discipline.

Students work in teams of between eight to ten people, when undertaking face-to-face problem-based learning, and have a tutor who facilitates the problem-based learning team. In PBLonline working in smaller groups of four to six students is much more effective, as will be discussed in later chapters. If a unit is designed in this way first of all, the focus is on what it is students will learn through the problems rather than focusing on covering predetermined content. Further, the students guide the learning, working out what it is that they need to know and understand in order to manage the situation effectively. A problem or scenario is the starting point for learning

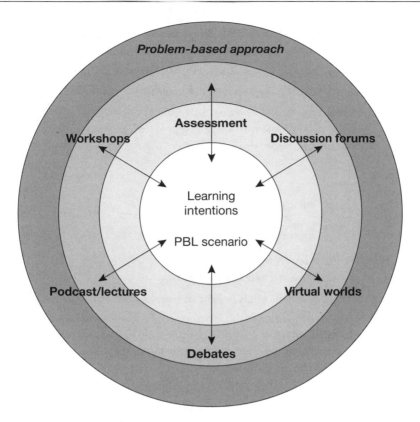

Figure 1.1 Problem-based curricula model

Week	1	2	3	4	5	6	7	8	9	10	11	12
Seminar 2 hours per week	Identify learning needs	Peer teaching	Synthesis									→
Problem		Scenario A			Scenario B		Scenario C			Scenario E		
Resources to support PBL	Lecture workshop	Laboratory discussion	Debate forum									→

Figure 1.2 A 12-week module/unit designed using problem-based learning

---

Box 1.3 Example of the PBL process for one problem over three seminars

Seminar 1: Identify learning needs

1   Study the scenario; asking *what* are the problems or issues?

2   Identify what you need to know to solve the problem
    – what do I need to know to solve the problems or issues?
    – where can I find information to help me solve the problems or issues?

3   Set an overall goal.

4   Identify corporate learning needs.

5   Allocate learning needs.

Seminar 2: Peer teaching

1   Peer teaching of researched knowledge.

2   Reassessment of overall goals in light of learning.

Seminar 3: Synthesis

Formulation of an action plan for resolving or managing the problem which may be in the form of, for example:

- a proposal   – a script
- a pamphlet   – a care plan
- a fact sheet   – a learning package
- a business plan   – an oral and/or written presentation

---

and this should comprise a query, puzzle and challenge to the students. In practice, the seminars over the 3 weeks would comprise the following focus and activities, outlined in Box 1.3

The example in Box 1.3 is one that has been the basis for the design of many face-to-face curricula, but it is also a useful foundation for designing PBLonline. This is because there is a tendency when devising online programmes to focus on the content that is to be covered rather than the activities and process of learning. By beginning with content coverage PBLonline is more likely to become a content covering resource pack rather than a space in which students are encouraged to wrestle with knowledge. If instead courses or programmes are developed by considering learning intentions, what it is that we wish students to learn, the focus will then be on problem-based learning activities rather than being driven by content.

The shift to PBLonline

The nature and process of interactive media has changed considerably over the last few years. Britain and Liber have noted that considerable effort has been expended on the development of managed learning environments rather than the pedagogy of such development (Britain and Liber, 2004: 8). The objective of combining problem-based learning and interactive media is in itself complex. Terms such as 'computer mediated problem-based learning' and 'online problem-based learning' have been used to define forms of problem-based learning that utilize computers in some way. However, this is problematic since it offers little indication about the ways in which computers are being used, the areas of interaction of the students, the quality of the learning materials or the extent to which any of these fit with problem-based learning (see for example, Barrow's (2002) discussion of distributed problem-based learning). Furthermore, there are other issues which need to be addressed, such as developing tutors' online facilitation capabilities, providing some synchronous events to support students, encouraging collaborative interactive participation and finding ways of engaging students who seldom participate in the online problem-based learning team.

There has also been much criticism, in the last decade, about interactive media environments that fail to create effective settings for learning (Noble, 2001; Reeves, 2002; Oliver and Herrington, 2003). One of the reasons for this has been because the focus in interactive media environments has been on technological rather than pedagogical design. There have been suggestions of a need for re-engineering the concept of learning design rather than just a simplistic repackaging of course content into interactive media formats (see, for example, Collis, 1997). Further, as Oliver and Herrington (2003) argue:

> In learning environments that support knowledge construction learners need to be exposed to a variety of resources and to have choices in the resources that they use and how they use them. An important aspect of resource development is to provide content that provides them with perspectives from a multitude of sources . . . The materials need not all be on-line.
>
> (Oliver and Herrington, 2003: 15)

In this text I use the term PBLonline as a generic term because it captures that vast variety of ways in which problem-based learning is being used synchronously and asynchronously, on campus, or at a distance.

Further it represents the idea that students learn through web-based materials including text, simulations, videos and demonstrations, and resources such as chatrooms, message boards and discussion forums as well as environments that have been purpose-built for problem-based learning.

Confusion and PBLonline

There is a sense of confusion or disjunction relating to using PBLonline and many people find it difficult to understand why it might be important to adopt this approach. Many of those I have spoken with argue against it since they believe the importance of problem-based learning lies in the face-to-face contact and small group work that students participate in through this approach. The reasons those struggling with the idea of PBLonline seem to argue against it are because they:

- can't see the point of PBLonline;
- prefer teaching face-to-face anyway;
- see it as being a lot more work;
- believe that curriculum design for PBLonline is complex and troublesome;
- dislike the idea of working in 3D virtual worlds as it introduces identity issues that feel unsafe;
- believe facilitating PBLonline is risky and precarious;
- consider that using games and play in PBLonline is not part of how learning at university should be, particularly in professional education.

The advantages that are often missed when linking problem-based learning and online learning are:

1   Changes in university cultures (such as split site campuses and universities with large student numbers) mean that PBLonline offers students space to learn in teams even though they may be dispersed geographically.
2   PBLonline creates a new type of learning community that is different from real time problem-based learning teams.
3   It is sometimes easier to challenge and confront peers through computer mediated problem-based learning than it is to do so face-to-face. It has been argued that computer mediated communication can provide more intense communication than face-to-face teams, where the lack of social pressure and the greater freedom to express views without struggling for the right of audience enabled participants to react to the content, and not the author, with more reflective and effective communications (Henri and Rigault, 1996: 10).
4   PBLonline often provides more opportunity for 'reflective and thoughtful analysis and review of earlier contributions' (Kaye, 1992: 17).
5   PBLonline can help students to use team conferences as an additional central communication space, as a place for sharing and examining individual perspectives and as a place to manage the work and administration of the team interaction.

The increasing adoption of problem-based learning and the growth in online learning each reflect the shift away from teaching as a means of transmitting information, towards supporting learning as a student-generated activity. This is not to imply that teachers are not required in PBLonline, but rather that their role is altered; existing skills need to be adapted and new skills adopted to support students in learning in virtual environments. As mentioned above, problem-based learning exists in many guises. Salmon (2002) refers to the increasing web of ever more sophisticated networked technologies. Combining the two approaches increases the number of possibilities, but this plethora of combinations offers potential for confusion, but reasons for combining them can be broken down into ten categories:

(1) Problem-based learning has been used successfully face-to-face and using PBLonline offers more flexibility for students
There is a sense that PBLonline does offer students more opportunity to learn in different times and spaces than more traditional face-to-face problem-based learning. However, forms of PBLonline that are provided as part of campus modules, so that they are blended, are largely less popular that face-to-face problem-based learning. Yet students still like the flexibility of both!

(2) It is seen as an innovative approach for using in the context of distance learning
There have been many innovative models of distance learning, beginning perhaps with the Open University. What is possibly different about PBL-online compared with other formulations of distant learning is the emphasis and requirement for students to learn (and possibly be assessed) in teams.

(3) Staff feel that a blended approach to problem-based learning would enhance both the pedagogical and technological experience of students
There is a sense that the underlying pedagogy of problem-based learning can enhance the way in which online learning is used. For example, there is still a tendency to implement online learning without always considering the impact on the curriculum and on the students' experience. Implementing PBLonline does prompt consideration of the roles of staff and students and how learning is to be constructed and by whom.

(4) It is seen as an approach that works well for interprofessional learning
While some forms of problem-solving learning have been used with interprofessional learning there is relatively little evidence that PBLonline works particularly well unless students have worked using face-to-face problem-based learning first. However, much of the success in any form of PBLonline, is in setting it up effectively and developing scenarios that work, and particularly in this case, challenge disciplinary boundaries and professional practices.

*(5) Increasing student numbers has led to a belief that online facilitation,
rather than face-to-face facilitation, could be more effective*
Teaching students and providing content by depositing it in a virtual learning
environment may provide more students more access to more information.
Institutions such as the Open University do teach many students worldwide
through online learning. However, PBLonline does require a different
pedagogy from many of the current forms of online learning. This is because
the responsibility for deciding what and how it is learned rests with the
students and the role of staff is in supporting them in this, thus facilitation
and small groups (four to six) is vital to ensure PBLonline is effective.

*(6) To provide a means of integrating diverse learning resources through
one teaching approach*
Although there is an increasing tendency to integrate diverse learning
resources, such 'multi inclusion curricula' are the kind of curricula which are
designed to enable students to cover a large body of knowledge and develop
key skills, whilst providing a wide variety of opportunities for learning. These
kinds of curricula are invariably designed to meet the requirements of multiple
stake holders; students, government, professional bodies, health service
consortia and employers. There is a sense that 'multi inclusion' curricula can
offer too much choice, so that ultimately the incoherence and diversity created
for the students through them can become disabling rather than enabling.

*(7) As a means of promoting and enhancing collaborative learning beyond
the classroom experience*
A number of PBLonline programmes and modules have been developed in
order to provide support for students beyond the classroom. For example,
Ronteltap (2006) and te Winkel *et al.* (2006) have created innovative new
learning spaces for students and developed new bespoke virtual learning
environments at the request of students on PBLonline modules.

(8) To reduce students' isolation and provide more support
PBLonline is not an approach that can guarantee to reduce isolation and
provide more support. Although PBLonline can provide supportive learning
spaces for students, particularly in blended modules, work by Bayne (2005a),
although not specifically relating to PBLonline found that many students
experience considerable isolation in online courses.

*(9) As a means of offering students more learning choices about what, when
and how they learn*
As mentioned above with regard to multi inclusion curriculum, PBLonline
can offer more choice to students, but there is also the danger with too much
flexibility that students choose not to engage with the learning and choose not
to work effectively as a team. Thus, what is vital is that PBLonline is designed

and thought through effectively and is both technologically and pedagogically sound.

(10) As a way of engaging students in learning tasks to fit with their social networking practices, particularly those such as 3D virtual worlds, mobile learning and social networking tools
Although many people who are beginning to use PBLonline aspire to engage with Web 2.0 and Web 3.0 technologies, to date there is relatively little, what I have termed Second Life problem-based learning occurring (see, for example, Savin-Baden, 2007). However, there is growth and interest in this area.

Models of problem-based learning and their fit with online learning

As with most innovations change is rapid, yet the change is not just about the pedagogy but also the discipline, arena and practice. Some of the types of problem-based learning, which are illustrated below, are possibly more flexible in their pedagogy and approach, and fit better with PBLonline than some of the more bounded models of problem-based learning. For further discussion on these different approaches see de Graaff and Kolmos (2003). However, it will be argued in Chapter 6 that we need to see PBLonline as a set of different constellations that because of their composition affect the way in which PBLonline is practiced. Nevertheless, there were some early models that also emerged in the 1980s that appeared to be more flexible than those offered by University of Maastricht, Netherlands and McMaster University in Canada. For example, Boud argued that problem-based learning could be seen in a variety of ways and suggested eight characteristics of many problem-based learning courses (Boud, 1985):

1   An acknowledgement of the base of experience of learners.
2   An emphasis on students taking responsibility for their own learning.
3   A crossing of boundaries between disciplines.
4   An intertwining of theory and practice.
5   A focus on the processes of knowledge acquisition rather than the products
6   A change in staff role from that of instructor to that of facilitator.
7   A change in focus from staff assessment of outcomes of learning, to student self and peer assessment.
8   A focus on communication and interpersonal skills so students understand that in order to relate their knowledge, they require skills to communicate with others, skills which go beyond their area of technical expertise.

Later, Walton and Matthews (1989) broadened this approach further and argued that problem-based learning should be understood as a general educational strategy rather than merely a teaching approach. They suggested that for problem-based learning to be present, three components must be able to be differentiated:

- Essential characteristics of problem-based learning that comprised curricula organization around problems rather than disciplines, an integrated curriculum and an emphasis on cognitive skills.
- Conditions that facilitated problem-based learning such as small groups, tutorial instruction and active learning.
- Outcomes that were facilitated by problem-based learning such as the development of skills and motivation, together with the development of the ability to be life-long learners.

Both models suggested by Boud (1985) and Walton and Matthews (1989) are broad enough to be adaptable to PBLonline, but a more recent model emerged in the early 2000s.

A problem a day

This approach was developed at Republic Polytechnic, Singapore (O'Grady and Alwis, 2002) and is termed the 'one-day one-problem approach'. Students thus spend one whole day working on a single problem. Over the course of a week students will work on five different, but related, problems. The day occurs as follows:

- In the morning students receive a problem scenario.
- Students with the help of a tutor in five groups of five (total of 25 students in a class) examine the problem and clarify what it is they do and do not know, and formulate possible hypotheses.
- Groups identify learning issues they will investigate and employ research strategies to collect relevant information.
- During the middle of the day the groups of five meet individually with the tutor to discuss their progress.
- The groups develop an outcome for the problem and present their findings to the other four groups of five and the tutor for evaluation.
- Groups discuss, defend and justify their outcomes and reflect on the way they have learnt in their groups.
- Students are assessed individually for their learning and record key learning milestones in their learning journal.

This mirrors many formats adopted by other tutors in the problem-based learning community, but it is condensed into one day. The authors argue that this approach has been adopted so that 'students would learn highly technical skills and subject matter so they can immediately enter into specific professional occupations and apply these skills with very little additional training, but at the same time be able to adapt to the quickly changing technological landscape' (O'Grady and Alwis, 2002). While this is a relatively new approach it would seem well suited to be adapted to PBLonline. Although this might prove difficult with distance modules across some time zones it would work well for rural community studies, such as that used by Reagan *et al.* (2001). The Faculty of Medicine and Dentistry at the University of Western Australia took 130 medical and 45 dental students, 4 weeks into the first year of their programme, to a country town for a week. The aim was for the students to learn about rural life and health and, in particular, what promotes, and detracts from, health. Working in groups and with the contact details of only one person in the town, the students were asked to research a subpopulation within the town (e.g. youth, elderly, cultural groups). This innovative approach to problem-based learning, the Rural Week, received highly positive feedback from students, academic tutors and the community.

These three models of problem-based learning are ones that challenge the linearity of many of the earlier models of face-to-face problem-based learning. It could be suggested that some of my early models should be cited here, but these are discussed in detail in Chapter 6.

Conclusion

Problem-based learning is an approach that continues to change and evolve and the shift to PBLonline has brought with it diverse ways of using different foci and a variety of design. The different approaches to problem-based learning that have been used face-to-face will both guide and inform the way problem-based learning is used in online settings. However, the emergence of Web 2.0 technologies and the focus on social networking along with networked learning will mean that PBLonline is likely to evolve behind the face-to-face approaches. Some of the current forms of PBLonline will therefore be considered in Chapter 2.

Note

1   The word team is used throughout the book to denote a group of people who work together with a common purpose, a limited membership and the power to make decisions. Teams have a focus, a set of team rules and are time limited. The term team is more appropriate than group to denote what occurs in most problem-based learning seminars because there is a focus, a remit and much of the learning that occurs evolves through the ways in which the team make decisions about what and how they learn within agreed or contracted deadlines.

Chapter 2

Forms of problem-based learning online

Introduction

This chapter will explore the challenges of using problem-based learning and forms of online learning together and will examine the relationship between them. In particular, it will analyse the differing formulations of problem-based learning online that are available. This chapter explains the particular types on offer and illustrates these with examples from around the world. However, it is clear that there are relatively few courses that use PBLonline, and fewer still that use it as an overarching component of a programme. However, it is important to consider the relationship between PBLonline and current conceptions of online learning, so that reflecting on the following questions may be a helpful starting point at the beginning of this chapter:

• How are you using online learning now?
• What are your concerns about using PBLonline?
• What do you see as the challenges?

PBLonline: a basic overview

The concept of problem-based learning online places it pedagogically in a collaborative online environment and thus it has a number of advantages over models mentioned earlier. While many of the current models of online education focus on teacher-centred learning, PBLonline needs to be focused on a team-led discourse centred on building the teams' capabilities, knowledges and understandings. In practice, this means that students need to work together online to identify their own learning needs and foci, rather than seeing their learning as being tutor-led or moderator-guided. The kind of discourse that needs to emerge in PBLonline spaces mirrors the characteristics of discourse suggested by Scardemalia and Bereiter (1994) who argued for: in-depth understanding, inquiry as a quest for understanding, and a conception of learning that included students, teachers, administrators, researchers, curriculum designers and assessors. The impact of the inclusion of these characteristics means that learners and facilitators may take on different roles in the course of a collaborative learning situation, which again brings online education of this sort in line with the dialogic nature of problem-based learning. Before ways are suggested as to how this might be achieved in practice, it is first important to define PBLonline and offer suggestions of how it might be implemented.

A broad definition of PBLonline

Problem-based learning online is defined here as students working in teams of four to six on a series of problem scenarios that combine to make up a module or unit that may then form a programme. Students are expected to work collaboratively to solve or manage the problem. Students will work in real-time or asynchronously, but what is important is that they work together. Synchronous collaboration tools are vital for the effective use of PBLonline because tools such as Chat, shared whiteboards, video conferencing and group browsing are central to ensuring collaboration within the problem-based learning team.

Students may be working at a distance or on campus, but they will begin by working out what they need to learn to engage with the problem situation. This may take place through a shared whiteboard, conferring or an email discussion group. What is also important is that students have both access to the objectives of the module and also the ability to negotiate their own learning needs in the context of the given outcomes. Facilitation occurs through the tutor having access to the ongoing discussions without necessarily participating in them. Tutors also plan real-time sessions with the PBLonline team in order to engage with the discussion and facilitate the learning.

For students the shift to new forms of learning, different from more traditional didactic approaches they have experienced in school and further education, is often challenging. The introduction of PBLonline introduces students to two new elements of learning. This has an impact not only on the problem-based learning and online learning, but also on other forms of learning within the curriculum. There are few curricula where problem-based learning is used as the only approach to learning and increasingly students have to manage not only the interplay of knowledge across modules but also different approaches to learning. However, there are also issues about the reasons for using PBLonline in the first place. For example, it is questionable as to whether there is value in using real-time PBLonline for students undertaking the same programme at the same university, unless it is because of long distances between students located at different campus sites who are all using the same problem-based learning scenario. Questions also need to be asked about whether having asynchronous teams add something different to PBLonline. Certainly, in distance education, across time zones and campus sites, this would be useful and suit different students' lives and working practices. Yet this raises problems about how cooperative and collaborative it is possible to be, in terms of sharing learning and ideas, and developing forms of learning that are genuinely dialogic in nature.

Designs in practice

Table 2.1 delineates some of the current PBLonline courses from around the world and locates them in terms of type. An explanation of each one is presented below.

Single module online at distance

These modules are predominantly designed as 1–12 week stand-alone modules that have been developed for a particular reason and with a particular focus. These have been designed, often, because of a specific need or as a result of student demand. These types are normally very successful, well supported and valued by students. Invariably they occur towards the end of a degree programme or as a stand alone postgraduate module. The following four examples illustrate some of these issues.

Jones *et al.* (2006) developed the notion of Virtual Clinics as a means of bringing practice-based learning opportunities to doctors studying at a distance on the MSc/PG Diploma in Sport and Exercise Medicine (SEM) at the University of Bath, UK. This programme already utilized asynchronous discussion and the authors wished to develop their use of online learning further. A pilot problem-based learning activity was designed using Moodle and a blend of synchronous and asynchronous discussion. In practice, this occurred in three two-hour synchronous meetings and two one-week asynchronous discussions over a two week period. The aim of the pilot was to explore the possibilities for designing and implementing PBLonline for clinical practice in a module about Sports Injuries and Rehabilitation. In practice, the authors implemented PBLonline, which included:

1   Resources, namely the problem scenario; a set of resources/artefacts that supported and added context to the problem, and a series of activities for engaging students.
2   Different forms of mediated communication.

Luck and Norton (2004) implemented a PBLonline module for Early Years Education and Care Managers at Liverpool Hope University, UK. The module focused on five scenarios over 12 weeks such as, 'You have taken over as the Managers of a Super Educare setting and implement changes in marketing and positioning of the organization. Why?' These provided the

Table 2.1 Designs in practice

Type of PBLOnline	Authors	Description	Discipline	Length
Single module online at distance	Jones et al. (2006)	MSc/PGDip	Sport and Exercise Medicine	24 weeks with 4 × 2 weeks of PBL across this period
	Luck and Norton (2004)	Undergraduate	Nursery Management	12 weeks
	Poikela et al. (2007)	Undergraduate	Physiotherapy placement module	8 weeks
	Lee (2006)	Undergraduate	Nursing	9 weeks
	Lycke et al. (2006)	Undergraduate	Medicine	12 weeks
Single module blended (campus and distance)	Savin-Baden and Gibbon (2006)	Undergraduate	Nursing	12 weeks
	Beaumont and Chew (2006)	Undergraduate	Information Systems	8 weeks
	Hmelo-Silver et al. (2006)	E-Step	Teacher Education	12 weeks
	Donnelly (2006)	PGDip	Diploma in Higher Education	12 weeks
Blended programmes	Poikela et al. (2007)	Undergraduate	Business Administration	16 weeks
	Poikela et al. (2007)	Undergraduate	Physiotherapy Placement module	3 year degree
	Stewart and Galea (2006)	Undergraduate	Plant Pathology/Entomology course	3 × 12 weeks
Content management systems for PBLonline	te Winkel et al. (2006) Ronteltap (2006)	Undergraduate Undergraduate	Psychology Cross University	
	Stewart et al. (2007)	PBLi Challenge FRAP	Cross Universities	

main learning opportunities for students. The problems were supplemented by guest speakers (videoed for the e-learners), group meetings with the tutor (delivered as simultaneous 'chat' online), and seminar activities or e-tivities. These latter activities were asynchronous for the e-learners using discussion forums on the VLE (virtual learning environment). The module was assessed by one formative and two summative group assignments (40 per cent), and one formative and one summative individual report (60 per cent).

Poikela *et al.* (2007) introduced PBLonline in the context of a physiotherapy programme at Mikkeli University of Applied Sciences, Savonlinna, Finland. Worldwide it is common for health and social care degrees in higher education to use practice or fieldwork placements in order to provide professional training for the students. Poikela *et al.* (2007) used PBLonline as a means of developing collaboration between physiotherapy students, teachers and supervisors during clinical placement periods. The online delivery took the form of using the virtual learning platform Moodle for asynchronous communication, and personal desktop conferencing software called Marratech (www.marratech.com) for synchronous communication. The undergraduate physiotherapist degree programme has been an integrated problem-based learning curriculum since 1998. Academic study units alternate with practical training periods in related content areas, both of which have been designed to enhance the integration of academic and clinical learning. Since the development project was launched in 2005, a range of electronic resources and online discussion tools has been introduced for the staff and the students. For example, physiotherapy students can choose between face-to-face and online tutorials, depending on their own needs during the period in question.

At the University of Dundee, UK, Lee (2006) examined the effectiveness of using problem-based learning as an online learning activity within an undergraduate distance learning module for practising specialist nurses. The 20 students on the programme were qualified nurses with a remit for infection control in a wide variety of settings, who wanted to complete a degree in conjunction with a specialist practitioner qualification in infection control. The module was supported by the use of a virtual learning environment. The evaluation of this support found online problem-based learning to be valuable in achieving the learning outcomes of the module by promoting development of expertise within an online community of practice. The role of problem-based learning in facilitating development of a community of practice is examined and a framework to guide its use proposed. Initially the module was designed to be run face-to-face, but then a decision was made to offer it exclusively in distance learning format, with the aim of targeting nurses across the UK and abroad. In practice, students were provided with a paper-based workbook and text book, with additional resources being provided via WebCT. The module comprised three problem-based learning scenarios over 9 weeks. An assignment surgery was provided for students along with a café forum, which enabled students to ask staff specific questions.

In Norway, Lycke *et al.* (2006) describe a 6-year medical education programme, which has integrated problem-based learning at all study levels. Staff believed that online communication would be a useful means of contact with students during their clinical period and help students to integrate clinical experiences with on-campus learning. Further, they believed it was important to equip doctors of the future with skills in information and communication technologies (ICT). PBLonline was introduced for students in the fifth year of their 6-year medical programme, when they were in clinical practice, geographically distributed to hospitals and general practices all over south-east Norway. During their clinical placement the students were to meet online twice weekly to manage the same problem scenario. This structure was familiar from their previous problem-based learning experiences on campus. Communication was to be synchronous (real time) with each session lasting for 30 to 45 minutes. After the students returned to campus, problem-based learning was continued face-to-face. The groups and their tutors were the same for the PBLonline and for the problem-based learning activities.

Single module blended (campus and distance)

These modules seem to be an increasingly popular way of using PBLonline worldwide, not only because of the rising use of online learning in universities and the wish to use it effectively, but also a desire to make online learning more student-centred. The extent to which these are on campus or at a distance varies considerably, but what is common across these modules is the desire to provide students with both flexibility and support, while also challenging them to develop independence in inquiry. The four examples below have adopted very different approaches and are from diverse disciplines. What is common to all of them is the focus of face-to-face seminars being a major support for the online sessions.

Hmelo–Silver *et al.* (2006) developed the eSTEP system, which is an online problem-based learning environment that provides undergraduate preservice teachers with an opportunity to engage with learning sciences concepts by using video cases as contexts for collaborative lesson redesign. The reasons for moving to PBLonline was because several different paper problem scenarios were used with only one roving facilitator and six to seven groups of students in the same room, which the authors believed did not reflect the world of the classroom. The facilitator found it difficult to work with several groups at the same time, and furthermore staff felt that students had difficulty in identifying valuable learning issues because of their limited prior knowledge of learning sciences and pedagogy.

The eSTEP system consists of three components:

1   The online learning sciences hypertext book, the Knowledge Web.
2   A library of video cases that present examples of classroom practice. These cases presented opportunities for both discussion and the redesign of instruction depicted in the cases. The video cases were indexed to the Knowledge Web, helping students identify fruitful learning issues.
3   A virtual learning environment (VLE) that provided resources and tools.

In practice, each block of eSTEP programme comprises three to four scenarios that each last 2–3 weeks, and the activities are illustrated below in Table 2.2.

Savin-Baden and Gibbon (2006) reported on a project that took place across schools of nursing at four UK Universities. Students Online in Nursing Integrated Curricula (SONIC) was developed to provide students with interactive problem-based learning scenarios that encouraged independent learning and student inquiry. Web-based resources supported each of the scenarios for second-year students in a problem-based learning module. The SONIC website uses standard web technology and Flash Player™ components that are available on the project website, as well as in each University's virtual learning environment. The impetus for the project came from a desire to support nursing students in their learning. Previous quality reviews of nursing education had indicated that students' knowledge of anatomy and physiology was generally regarded as poor. The project provided Flash

Table 2.2 eSTEP activities

Activity	Description	Modality
STEP 1	Study video case	Individual, online
STEP 2	Record observations and initial proposals in online personal notebook that guides students towards relevant lesson features	Individual, online
STEP 3	View other student proposals	Collaborative, online
STEP 4	Identify concepts to explore for redesign	Collaborative, face-to-face
STEP 5	Conduct and share research	Collaborative, online
STEP 6	Collaborative lesson design	Collaborative, online
Poster session	Groups present project to class	Collaborative, face-to-face
STEP 7	Explanation and justification of group product	Individual, online
STEP 8	Reflection	Individual, online

Source: Hmelo et al., 2006: 66.

Player™ based physiology resources as a different approach to learning, to improve students' expertise in this area of concern. The website materials comprise five scenarios, two adult, one child, one mental health and one for learning disabilities, matching the corresponding undergraduate nursing programmes. Each scenario is studied within the first module of the second year (termed 'branch programme') and, following pilot studies with groups of approximately 15 students per scenario, the resources are now embedded within each curriculum. The students meet face-to-face in problem-based learning teams, study the scenario on the website and then use the website resources to support their learning. The problem scenarios remain on an open website at all times and, depending upon the programme, students meet 2–3 times per week over 3–4 weeks to engage with the scenarios and to decide how they will manage the problem situation with which they have been presented.

In contrast, Donnelly designed and implemented a staff development module at Dublin Institute of Technology, Ireland. It is a 10-week module entitled 'Designing E-Learning', which is delivered using a blend of face-to-face and online problem-based learning. Module participants are drawn from very diverse fields and have spent varying lengths of time as lecturers. There is also a wide range in knowledge and experience about both e-learning and problem-based learning. All participants are self-selecting and choose to come on the course. A specific approach was taken to the design and delivery of this module by using problem-based learning as the dominant pedagogical model. The online delivery component and support of the module is in the Online Learning Environment, WebCT. The aim of the module 'Designing E-Learning' is to enable the participants (lecturers, librarians and educational technologists), through a blended learning approach of problem-based learning, to become aware of the practicalities of designing, delivering, supporting and evaluating an online module in their own subject disciplines.

Beaumont and Chew (2006) developed an unusual example of PBLonline that was undertaken within and across Singapore and the UK, sponsored by the British Council and Temasek Polytechnic, Singapore. The project was to explore and analyse how students used ICT to support problem-based learning. The technologies used comprised both synchronous and asynchronous tools. Synchronous tools included Integrated Services Digital Network (ISDN) video conferencing, Webcam video conferencing and synchronous chat. They used a portal that provided an asynchronous threaded discussion forum, drop-box and peer and self-assessment tools. Each problem-based learning team consisted of four undergraduate Information Systems students in the UK and four polytechnic students in Singapore. The problem-based learning scenario lasted 6 weeks, including 1 week for preparation and presentation, and consisted of a computer network security scenario, involving both theory and practical work. Students were required to identify security risks and threats to the scenario's network, and then design a new, securer infrastructure. The sub-teams of UK and Singapore students held local face-to-face meetings in addition to using other communication media.

Blended programmes

There are relatively few blended PBLonline programmes (that is full degree programmes that are linked together by modules with a clear PBLonline philosophy across them all). Most staff using PBLonline tend to adopt it in one module and then extend it module by module across a whole programme. Few programmes have been designed from the outset as wholly PBLonline, although there are a number presently under development at Coventry University, UK. Those blended programmes that do exist retain the feature of single blended modules with a focus on support provided through face-to-face seminars, yet with all of them the type, time and structures vary. Yet there appear to be four reasons for the development of PBLonline programmes:

- to provide student support;
- to help students develop independence in inquiry through online systems;
- to facilitate problem-solving capabilities;
- to build effective online teams.

Stewart and Galea (2006) describe the development of problem-based approaches to training students in plant disease diagnosis. The programme is for undergraduate plant pathology students at Massey University, New Zealand and the University of Queensland, Australia. The three examples the authors offer of PBLonline comprise presenting students with a problem scenario and asking them to solve it, getting students to construct their own problem scenarios, and using an electronic format as a guide, recording, and feedback tool during a real-life diagnostic exercise. The first of these is a scenario-based "game" approach where students are expected to analyse a problem. The second example involves students constructing scenarios in order to understand the processes involved in plant disease diagnosis. Special software was available for both these purposes called 'DIAGNOSIS for CROP PROBLEMS', which allowed a series of multimedia tasks and observations to be worked through or constructed by students. In 2007, this software was retired and replaced with similar lessons constructed in PBL-Interactive. The third example explores use of software (Challenge FRAP, from 2008 known as Challenge Workbook) as an 'electronic workbook and guide' while trying to solve a real diagnostic problem both in the field and in the laboratory (Stewart et al., 2007). Here students are presented with a real or artificial scenario and are asked to assess the problem and give treatment recommendations.

A different approach was taken by Poikela *et al.*, 2007, who describe the integration of Web 2.0 technologies for creating a common information base for groups. This innovation was undertaken at Ikaalinen Business School, University of Applied Sciences, Pirkanmaa Polytechnic, Finland. The focus was to create an innovative learning environment combining problem-based learning and Web 2.0. First, the existing business studies undergraduate degree was redesigned as a problem-based programme. Then development of the common information base for groups was undertaken through using an asynchronous discussion forum and a wiki embedded in the Moodle learning management system. The students used the discussion forum for the development of ideas and for sharing and locating information. After using the discussion forum for 8 weeks the students started to use the wiki for information sharing. Initially students found the wiki confusing, difficult and time consuming, but it was ultimately recognized as more convenient, because information was better organized and easy to find.

The undergraduate physiotherapist degree programme in Savonlinna has been a blended programme since 2005. There is a clear PBLonline philosophy in the whole physiotherapy programme with face-to-face and online tutorial groups arranged in every module of the curriculum. Students can decide whether to study the whole degree programme, or some parts of it from distance, or if they want to stay at the campus. Additionally it is expected that all small-groups use asynchronous facilities like discussion forums (in Moodle or WebCT learning platform) for exchanging information search findings, posting learning documents and responding to each other between the tutorials. This blended learning has mainly been developed to meet the needs of students to work as teams in online tutorials, project and seminar work, in spite of the physical separation of distance and also to support open learning and collective knowledge building during the self-study phases between the tutorials.

Content management systems

A number of these types of developments have been created to support PBL-online. Whilst some are only websites that provide hints, tips and exemplars of scenarios, there are more developed content management systems available. The following three exemplars are probably the most sophisticated ones currently available and those in the Netherlands have take student feedback into account in their design and redesign.

PsyWeb

PsyWeb (te Winkel *et al.*, 2006) is a Learning Content Management System that aims to extend students' opportunities for individual knowledge construction during self-study. The system manages thousands of learning resources from the entire 4-year psychology curriculum. Rather than treating all resources alike, ten different categories of learning resources are identified: articles, book chapters, lectures, problems, videos, internet sites, e-chapters, electronic presentations, animations and interactive experiments. Integrated into the system is a set of instructional techniques to assist and enhance student learning activities. PsyWeb was developed to stimulate the elaboration process by using many diverse electronic learning resources. These resources support students not only in remembering the required information more successfully, but also in learning it more easily and applying it more appropriately. The authors suggest, rather than arguing that specific types of learning resource produce a given learning effect, that many of the categories of learning resources serve the same learning effect, and that a single category could serve many learning effects. Thus, students are encouraged to choose one category over another, based on their individual learning style and specific task requirements.

POLARIS

Problem-based learning is the main approach in all curricula at Maastricht University (UM), being Medicine, Health Sciences, Economics, Law, Psychology, Cultural Sciences and Knowledge Technology. Although every day educational practice varies, a few basic elements are present in all curricula. Starting from the same principled approach as Koschmann *et al.* (1996), Ronteltap and Eurelings (2002) evaluated several educational practices at Maastricht University. Ronteltap and Eurelings found a different set of problems. A continuously increasing number of students starting their studies at this university year on year led to students reporting a decreasing number of opportunities to meet and discuss their learning issues, and an increasing distance between students and tutors. Based on these findings, Ronteltap and Eurelings (2002) built POLARIS (Problem Oriented Learning and Retrieval Information System) to offer students an asynchronous communication tool that could extend discussions with tutors and peer students, and a shared work environment to submit written reports related to their learning issues. The communication tool was based on an analysis of how people learn in small groups. From the software perspective, it looked like a threaded discussion board. However, it was extended with specific functionality, focused on activities in small group learning (Ronteltap, 2006). The tool supported creative work and continuous improvement of ideas by writing, sharing, discussing, comparing, integrating, reorganizing and restructuring of information.

PBLi and Challenge FRAP

The Centre for Biological Information Technology at The University of Queensland (CBIT) has developed, in conjunction with Massey University, New Zealand, an interactive, problem-based learning software product (PBLi) that enables a virtual representation of real-life 'problems'. PBL-interactive (PBLi) is a software suite designed to enable teachers, lecturers and others working in training or education, to create and deliver interactive scenarios as an aid to problem-based or enquiry-based learning. It has designed PBLi to allow 'problem solvers' to interact with a problem, to record their response to the problem and to receive either instant or delayed online feedback, including formal assessment as appropriate. The CBIT has developed applications that enable horticultural scientists, farmers and students, for example, to engage online with complex real world problems such as the emergence of pests and diseases in crops and to diagnose the specific problem and then resolve it. It has also developed scenarios that deal with the sorts of real world problems that are encountered by social workers, engineers and medical practitioners among others (available at www.lsc. qld.gov.au/projects/3scenario.htm). A development of PBLi is the e-learning tool 'Challenge FRAP' (Form for the Recording of the Analysis of Problems). This is client-based public domain authoring software, which facilitates the use of scaffolding, the provision of progressive feedback and can promote student reflection at key decision-making points. It offers both the problem-based learning designer and learner a range of tools and templates that enable better design and learning opportunities. For more detail on this new initiative, see Stewart *et al.* (2007).

Conclusion

The shift to PBLonline has resulted in many and varied approaches to the development of problem-based learning in online settings. The studies here illustrate the diversity of formulations, structures and disciplines currently using PBLonline across the globe. Further, there is an increase in the development of software to support PBLonline and the use of it in modules is increasing year by year. However, to date there remain few blended degree programmes and even fewer PBLonline programmes at a distance – although there are already plans to design and implement such programmes. What is common across the stories of those who have implemented PBLonline are the mistakes and assumptions they have made in designing and delivering it, and it is these to which we turn next in Chapter 3.

Chapter 3

Common mistakes and assumptions

Introduction

Many in the field of problem-based learning have felt that it could be easily adapted to online environments, but have found this more difficult than they had envisaged. This chapter will explore the mistakes other have made and suggest alternative strategies. This chapter will also include reflections from experts in the field regarding their design decisions; choices and views about what they would do were they were attempting it again for the first time.

Problem-based learning, problem-solving and problem-solving learning

One of the biggest mistakes many people make in wanting to introduce PBLonline is assuming that problem-solving, problem-solving learning and problem-based learning are the same thing. Problem-based learning starts from the premise that students decide what it is they need to learn, they research and share the information and then synthesize it in order to manage the problem situation effectively. Problem-solving and problem-solving learning are different from this because the focus in these approaches is not just on solving the problem, but also there is an underlying assumption that the solution to the problem is already known. Further, a critical aspect of understanding *problem-solving* is seen as problem analysis. The most famous approach is that of Newell and Simon (1972) and a state-space analysis. The idea is that a problem solver searches through a problem space until she finds a solution, or fails to find one and gives up. However, it is important to note that problem-solving is a component of the problem-based approach and some disciplines put more emphasis on the problem-solving components of it than others. Whereas *problem-solving learning* is more than just finding a solution to a given problem, indeed it is the type of teaching many staff have been using for years. The focus is upon giving students a lecture or an article to read and then a set of questions based upon the information given. Students are expected to find the solutions to these answers and bring them to a

Table 3.1 Comparison of PBLonline and PSOnline

Method	Organization of knowledge	Forms of knowledge	Role of student	Role of tutor	Type of activity	Nature and size of group
Problem-based learning online	Open-ended situations and problems	Contingent and constructed	Active participants, independent critical inquirers	E-facilitator Enabler of opportunities for learning	Development of strategies to facilitate team and individual learning	4–6 students Knowledge creators
Problem-solving online	Step-by-step logical problem-solving through knowledge supplied by lecturer	Largely propositional but may also be practical	Problem-solver who acquires knowledge through bounded problem-solving	E-moderator A guide to the right knowledge and solution	Finding solutions to given problems	6–15 students Solutions finders

seminar as a focus for discussion. Problem scenarios here are set within and bounded by a discrete subject or disciplinary area. In some curricula students are given specific training in problem-solving techniques, but in many cases they are not. The focus in this kind of learning is largely upon acquiring the answers expected by the lecturer, answers that are rooted in the information supplied in some way to the students. Thus the solutions are always linked to a specific curricula content, which is seen as vital for students to cover in order for them to be competent and effective practitioners. The solutions are therefore bounded by the content and students are expected to explore little extra material other than that provided, in order to discover the solutions.

In practice then, PBLonline will look very different from problem-solving online in terms of the type of scenarios used, the role of the facilitator, and the experience for students, as exemplified in Table 3.1.

Assumptions

This section explores some of the common assumptions made about the shift to PBLonline.

It is easy to do

A number of colleagues spoke to me about moving to PBLonline some 10 years ago, and embarked on a blended approach. The initial difficulties they experienced were in designing suitable scenarios, but perhaps the biggest challenge was deciding as a team what it was they all meant by PBLonline, facilitation and the way in which the teams would operate. For example, Pirjo Vuoskoski, Mikkeli University of Applied Sciences, Savonlinna, Finland explained how she feels now:

> I really have to say, I love being a facilitator in PBL online. I like challenges, you see ☺. I love being a facilitator in PBL in general, but the online environment makes the job even more challenging and rewarding . . .

However, this was not how she felt to begin with:

> I thought it was something new, more fun but 'tricky' during that time. I became very interested but not yet fully devoted to the usage of ICT with PBL, because of the technical inflexibility. I didn't see the textual collaboration so effective. Maybe it was also because of my background as a therapist, I was missing especially the visual eye-contact and non-verbal-part of communication. I also had very strong doubts about my own technical skills.

Staff will facilitate it well

There is often an assumption that if you are experienced at face-to-face facilitation that the transitions to online facilitation will be relatively straight forward. This is not the case. This is because reading team interaction online is more complex than reading interactions in face-to-face discussion. Further, it is also a challenge to know how to position oneself as a facilitator, since the role of the PBLonline facilitator differs from that of an e-moderator.

Students will like it

There is a sense that PBLonline can give students more space to learn for themselves and more freedom from the life and times of campus. However, as with much online learning, the extent to which students engage with it depends on the students, the way they are equipped to use it, and perhaps most importantly of all whether they believe it is interesting and useful to them. Reports on students' perceptions about PBLonline vary, although it would seem that to date most students prefer blended PBLonline models to distance approaches. This however, may change as the problem-based learning community gains greater experience in this area.

Students are ahead of us and are familiar with the technology

There is often an assumption that because students belong to the X Generation they are all competent at using discussion boards, Skype and messaging. (People born between 1963 and 1978 are generally considered to be Generation X, but others use the term to describe anyone who was in their twenties at some time during the 1990s.) Although many students use social networking such as MySpace and Facebook, they often find the technology used through university VLEs seems both unfamiliar and clunky. Other students, whether mature or school leavers, may not play games or be able to do much more than use a search engine and email. For others it is important to use software students are familiar with, as Chris Beaumont at Liverpool Hope University, UK explained:

> I think it is also important to provide tools students are familiar with. When we provided synchronous chat facilities via the VLE, students wouldn't use it. They were familiar with MSN messenger, which had a much more usable interface and could be logged in automatically.

However, 'Generation C' is a term now being used to capture the idea that we live in an age of content producers. There is also a further shift to include not just content but context. For example, Cook (2007) has argued for the notion of Generation CX to capture this and Bruns (2007) has suggested that we are not in the realms of 'produsage'; a core activity of Generation C.

Engagement in the module will be high

As with most online learning the level of engagement not only depends on how well staff and students have been prepared for working in this way, but also on the cohort, the form of PBLonline, and the overall commitment of staff and students to learning in this way. PBLonline initiatives that have been prompted by students' requests have proved popular and the resources have been well utilized. For example, te Winkel *et al.* (2006) developed PsyWeb, at Erasmus University, Rotterdam to support students not only in remembering required information more successfully, but also in learning it more easily and applying it more appropriately. PsyWeb is a Learning Content Management System that aims to extend students' opportunities for individual knowledge construction during self-study. The system manages thousands of learning resources from the entire 4-year psychology curriculum. Rather than treating all resources alike, ten different categories of learning resources are identified: articles, book chapters, lectures, problems, videos, internet sites, e-chapters, electronic presentations, animations and interactive experiments. Ronteltap (2006) also explored student perspectives and developed a new tool for group communication in the context of learning. This tool, POLARIS, was developed at the Learning Lab at the University of Maastricht. It contains two components: a group environment *Knowledge Builder* in which information is exchanged, followed by subsequent feedback; and the personal environment *Knowledge Manager* in which the products of the collaboration can be manipulated and stored for later access.

Everyone will cope with the technology

Assuming that everyone will cope with the technology is the biggest mistake most people make, whether with PBLonline or any other form of online learning. Even if staff and students see themselves as technologically competent, the shift to PBLonline is still often a shock, as staff at Pirkanmaa Polytechnic – University of Applied Sciences, Ikaalinen, Finland found:

> The meeting online demanded more concentration than the face-to-face meetings, it was difficult to follow the conversation especially during the last meeting which was held in English. Because of the lack of non-verbal communication (facial expressions, movements, etc.) due to the missing video connection (to enable everybody to keep the connection without breaks through less burden on the lines) the conversation was found very difficult to follow.

No one will sabotage it

The issue of sabotage per se is rarely spoken of in online learning, while particular behaviours such as flaming and lurking are deemed as being unacceptable – which, as will be discussed in Chapter 4, probably need to be rethought in different and less negative terms. There is, however, evidence of sabotage occurring in face-to-face problem-based learning. Thus tutors who dislike problem-based learning and/or online learning are unlikely to support it and the same will be the case with students. As with face-to-face problem-based learning, ensuring that staff are committed to the development is vital. This kind of development can be an area of great sensitivity to tutors who have been experts in their disciplines and subjects for many years. Many tutors find changing their roles to be a complex and difficult process. The analogy of crossing the chasm (Moore, 1999, following Rogers, 1962) is a useful way of engaging with many of the issues related to implementing an innovation such as problem-based learning and dealing with tutor reactions to this new approach. Moore's work relates to the development and adoption of technology within companies. He argued that there is a chasm between two distinct marketplaces: an early market that tends to dominated by those keen to take it on board (early adopters), along with insiders who quickly see the benefit of the new development. The second marketplace is characterized by a range of people who ultimately want the benefits of the new technology but are slower to take it up and more cynical about its possibilities. What tends to occur is the emergence of a chasm between those in the early market and those in the later mainstream market. Crossing this chasm is an important focus for those involved in any innovation. However, it is more difficult to ensure student commitment but using warm-up scenarios that address issues of sabotage are a useful means of engaging with possible issues of sabotage at the outset, for example, those provided by Bayne in Chapter 5.

Anyone can facilitate it

Facilitation is different from moderation and it is generally better to have undertaken face-to-face problem-based learning before attempting PBL-online facilitation. This is because there is an initial tendency for inexperienced facilitators to interrupt or weave too much. For example, in face-to-face problem-based learning of student nurses, Wilkie (2004) found four approaches to facilitation present in the first year that the programme ran, but by later years most facilitators had adopted the fourth approach.

The approaches were:

- *Liberating supporter*: this approach was characterized by minimal facilitator intervention and promotion of self-directed learning, with the focus on content acquisition.

- *Directive conventionalist*: this group of facilitators retained control of both the material to be learned and the method by which students were expected to learn.
- *Nurturing socializer*: the approach was student-centred, nurturing and supportive with an emphasis on socializing students into 'good' standards (as defined by the facilitator) of nursing practice.
- *Pragmatic enabler*: this approach developed with experience as facilitators recognized that one style of facilitation did not meet the needs of all student teams and that the problem-based process was affected by factors such as student characteristics, the nature of the problem, frame factors and the amount of dialogue. Facilitators adopted this approach in an attempt to match the student-centred, self-directed nature of problem-based learning with the demands of the competency-driven pre-registration nursing programme.

Although there have been few studies to have explored approaches to facilitation in the context of PBLonline, it is likely that there will be similarities with Wilkie's findings.

It will be very popular and highly acclaimed

With any innovation it is those that are popular that tend to be highly acclaimed. Success will come with sound setup, planning, design, equipping of staff and students and excellent resources.

It is cheaper than face-to-face learning

Problem-based learning has a reputation for being more expensive than lecture-based learning, although there is little evidence to support this. For example, there is still much controversy, particularly with regard to library costs, classroom allocation and tutor support for problem-based learning. However, Mennin and Martinez-Burrola (1990) studied the cost of problem-based learning compared with conventional curricula and demonstrated only very small differences. They also found that in problem-based learning curricula 70 per cent of tutor time was in contact with students, while on conventional courses 70 per cent of tutor time was in preparation for contact with students. From this it would seem that funding comparisons between problem-based learning courses and other courses might just be a question of emphasis. As with face-to-face problem-based learning, PBLonline requires support for set-up and training of staff (see, for example, Savin-Baden and Major, 2004, Chapter 10) but is no more expensive than other forms of online learning.

It can been done easily in large groups

PBLonline can be difficult and problematic in large groups. Those who have attempted to run PBLonline teams of over 30 students have found this complex and troublesome. Adopting small teams within a large cohort works more effectively with the facilitator working across the teams. Chris Beaumont at Liverpool Hope University, UK explained:

> I think the most problematic point we came across when starting out with PBL Online was caused by multiple tutors providing different information, and having different expectations about what students were required to do/produce. Our context had tutors (and students) in different countries. We had not foreseen the difficulties in clarification that students needed.

Mistakes

The mistakes voiced here reflect the perspectives of those from around the globe who have implemented PBLonline.

Moderation rather than facilitation

Moderation may be defined in a number of ways and the relationship between moderation and facilitation will be discussed in detail in Chapter 5. Moderation is described by Salmon (2000) as the notion of presiding over a meeting, but also as something broader to refer to online teaching and facilitation. Yet facilitation is also multifaceted and can be seen as a series of different types with different agenda. For example, to date few debates have taken place about the nature and process of facilitation in problem-based learning. While the research and literature in these areas is growing there has still been relatively little discussion about what is being facilitated – whether it is students' understanding and enactment of problem-based learning, the team process, the process of learning, individual learning, or the achievement of the learning outcomes, and to what extent the tutor's ability to facilitate affects all these. However, this is discussed in-depth in Chapter 5.

Simplistic scenarios

Many colleagues have realized that complex messy scenarios are ones that work best. Straight forward and particularly linear scenarios generate little discussion and students quickly become bored. Several examples of scenarios that work effectively in PBLonline are provided in the Resources section of this book.

Considering lurking is a 'bad thing'

Lurking, reading or browsing without adding to the discussion has, to date, had a bad press. PBLonline is an approach where lurking needs to be seen differently and a new model of engagement is presented in detail in Chapter 5. However, it is important to note that lurking in PBLonline is not about a lack of engagement or a denial of responsibility, but is in fact often about students requiring space to think, time (sometimes) to get online, time to catch up with discussion threads and space to consider their position. As a result it is important that space is built into real time sessions as well as synchronous sessions to allow students 'lurking space'.

Discussion forums are enough

The focus on proprietary VLEs such as Blackboard has meant that the possibility and flexibility for PBLonline have been somewhat limited. As Beaumont suggested earlier, using systems that students are familiar with is vital. It is important to use real time events, such as MSN chat, but also to engage in activities such as learning in Second Life which can stimulate changes in the nature and process of both discussion and teamwork. For example, through using avatars in Second Life problem-based learning teams seem to develop a stronger sense of each others' identities and hence work more effectively as a team, than they do just in linear discussion forums.

Lots of provided reading is necessary

Provided reading is useful but in PBLonline too much material can distract students from focusing on their own learning needs. The result is that they fail to own the scenarios and focus on the facilitators' reading list, direction and agenda. Too much reading can also result in students using each other less as resources.

A good instructional management system will solve most problems

A study by Wegner *et al.* (1999) used a problem-based model to compare two groups of students undertaking a two-year advanced level curriculum design and evaluation programme. Both the experimental group and control group used problem-based learning. The control group used communication technology that included telephone, fax, email and research websites. Students in the experimental group utilized an instructional management system, namely *TopClass*. The findings indicated that the use of an instruction management system for the delivery of distance learning had a positive effect on the number of internet-based communications by students. This would seem to indicate that such systems, linked with problem-based learning, would promote inter-student communication more effectively than PBLonline without instructional management systems. However, the authors of this study did not appear to evaluate the problem-based learning component of this programme.

However, in terms of examining the pedagogy of PBLonline, perhaps it is also useful not just to look at designing the structure but also at designing the pedagogy.

Students will have the necessary software

There is an assumption with the rise of social networking that Generation X students and beyond are all highly computer literate and familiar with social networking tools. This is still not entirely the case. Students use their mobile phones, texting is the predominant mode of communication but not all students have high spec computers or broadband facilities at home. There are also often compatibility problems, as Chris Beaumont as Liverpool Hope University, UK explained:

> A further assumption, always problematic was the availability of software at student's homes. For example, recently one of our tutors has adopted use of Tablet PC and handwritten feedback. However, some students were unable to view the annotated MS Word documents because of software incompatibilities.

Face-to-face scenarios can just be put into a VLE and supported by a discussion board

In the context of problem-based learning there needs to be clarity about how scenarios are created so that they produce robust educational discussion, but perhaps different types of scenarios need to be used in online learning than in face-to-face problem-based learning. At one level the inter-linking of problem-based learning with virtual learning environments has brought creativity to problem-based learning and the development of innovative multimedia materials. Yet it is clear from much of the literature that this is not always the case, and the focus on the achievement of outcomes and tasks is already causing instead a narrowing of the definition of problem-based learning, and a certain boundedness about both the types of problem scenarios being adopted, and the actual way that problem-based learning is being used. As with most successful online learning, set-up, design, support and implantation is vital at the outset.

A case study provided by Maija Kärnä of Pirkanmaa Polytechnic, Finland illustrates many of the issues discussed above.

Case study

Background

Pirkanmaa Polytechnic – University of Applied Sciences has been using a problem-based curriculum since 2005 in business studies. Ongoing development of PBL curricula and new technical solutions to support PBL has continued since. During autumn 2006 a group of ten third-year students who were thoroughly familiar with PBL trialled Marratech software to facilitate online tutorial meetings.

Experiences

After three online sessions the students were asked to write a learning diary on their experiences. The following reflections were collated:

1   Technical problems including echo effect on the sound and getting disconnected during the meeting were the most common problems mentioned in the reports. However, although only two or three of the students experienced these problems they affected negatively on the learning experiences of all students.
2   The meeting online demanded more concentration than the face-to-face meetings, and it was difficult to follow the conversation, especially during the last meeting which was held in English. Because of the lack of non-verbal communication (facial expressions, movements, etc.) due to the missing video connection (to enable everybody to keep the connection without breaks through less burden on the lines) the conversation was found very difficult to follow.
3   There was a less vivid discussion during the online meetings than during the face-to-face tutorials. There was more 'lecturing' than real exchange of opinions. Some of the students commented that the shy ones were left aside as they were not active enough to demand a turn in the discussion. Even those who normally were relatively active in discussion reported that during the closing session they left things unsaid because they felt awkward working online.
4   Due to the sluggish discussion some of the students reported that the learning outcomes of the online session did not reach the same level as in face-to-face discussions. The amount of information searched for during the session was less than in normal face-to-face discussions. It was easier to hide behind the active ones and be quiet.
5   The discussion took more time than the face-to-face discussion and even then the students felt that there was too little time for the session.

Improvements suggested

a   Clear rules of behaviour are necessary to avoid several participants speaking at the same time. The mediator should keep the discussion very strongly under control. Also the role of the tutor to keep order was emphasized.

b   Technical problems must be eliminated more efficiently. Everybody involved should have a powerful enough net connection and good equipment including a high quality headset-microphone especially.

Conclusions

The following ideas are based on the reports of the students as well as on my own findings:

1   The online sessions worked especially well for the opening tutorial sessions. The whiteboard which could be used at the same time by all students for brainstorming and later arranging the ideas into groups worked really well. Work was efficient, and coordination, i.e. rules of the game, was found easily among the students.

2   Closing sessions were more difficult. As mentioned there was not enough discussion, what went on during the session was more like short lectures than exchange of opinions. The students reported that they needed more experience and clear rules for the discussion. They also reported that some students did not do their independent information searching as effectively as normally. It was easy to draw back and leave the discussion and the responsibility to others. Without the normal requirement to present a certain amount of information on the discussion forum or wiki area on the net (Moodle learning platform) during the week between the opening and closing sessions, the learning results would have been totally unsatisfactory. The latter is both the opinion of the more responsible students as well as the tutor's.

The students suggested that the Marratech online session would be especially well suited for the following situations:

- opening tutorial sessions;
- tutor-student assessment discussion sessions;
- as a group work tool for student groups working on an assignment;
- for lecturing, also from overseas, Marratech would enable the students to ask questions during the lesson and still work from home;
- occasionally and with a lot of rehearsing and clear rules for the closing tutorial sessions.

Conclusion

Many staff made mistakes that are similar to those made in the process of implantation of any innovation, although it seems that the technology definitely complicated things further. Perhaps the last word should come from Pirjo Vuoskoski, Mikkeli University of Applied Sciences, Savonlinna, Finland, who has been using PBLonline since 2005 and reflects upon the issues that occurred from the outset:

> Definitely we should have had more resources (time, technology and people involved) for preparing the programme and educating the students and staff members better. We had one day for educating students and staff how to use Marratech, Moodle/WebCT and cmaptools, and another half for explaining the background of elearning and eteaching for the staff in the autumn, just before we started. However, especially the staff members were not participating well. They were too busy and some of them were strongly resisting the change. This was occurring more in other departments like nursing, but affected the general atmosphere in health care campus, too. It aroused suspicions among students and staff (like, 'why we are the only ones using so much ICT?'), and caused envy in other departments (when we needed more technological facilities and time resources to start the pilot project, etc.). There is a need for much longer periods (several weeks, maybe even months) with a proper plan for student and staff training for the new learning and teaching environment, with the involvement of librarians and technicians from the very beginning – was the most important lesson learnt. This is maybe not the only mistake we have made, but definitely the biggest affecting serious challenges every day.

Chapter 4

Equipping staff and students for problem-based learning online

Introduction

This chapter will debunk some of the myths about facilitating PBLonline, and in particular the idea that has been seen by some as an easier (or more difficult) option than managing face-to-face facilitation. It will argue that one of the main differences in facilitating PBLonline compared with other forms of online learning is the need to focus on collaborative and dialogic learning. The chapter begins by examining ways of equipping staff and suggests that a useful starting point is to explore staff's own pedagogical stances and analyse the way they choose to position themselves as teachers, since this will this affect the way they locate themselves as PBLonline facilitators. The second section of Chapter 4 focuses on equipping students and presents a case study of two students' experiences, which provides powerful illustrations of some of the complexities of students' perspectives when learning in online teams.

Starting with ourselves

One of the central principles of facilitating PBLonline is that until we understand our own pedagogical stance if is difficult to operate effectively as a PBLonline facilitator. Thus until we understand our own views about teaching, our ideas about collaboration in online spaces and are able to consider the issues of student responsibility, it is difficult to locate ourselves in these complex spaces. How facilitators position themselves is relational and can be affected by a number of factors; it changes over both time and in relation to the problem-based teams that are being facilitated. Some of the more negative possibilities that staff experience are delineated below (for exemplars of this see Lycke *et al.*, 2006). For instance, it is worth considering whether you or a member of your team is feeling:

1   *Displaced*, no longer strongly located in one discipline and having to work inside and outside their area of expertise, resulting in ambivalence about both their role and its value.

2   *Repositioned,* so that they see PBLonline facilitation as a positive
    opportunity to reposition themselves as tutors, and are able to realign
    their pedagogical stances with their view of themselves as enablers of
    learning.
3   *Dislocated,* because they dislike problem-based learning since they feel
    unable to control the content and the learning in the way they felt they
    could in lecture-based forms of learning, or because of the disjunction
    they experienced as a result of their role change.

Therefore, a useful starting point is to ask yourself about how you see your
position as a facilitator in PBLonline:

How much guidance do I expect to give to the students?

How do I expect groups to work?

What do I believe are the students' roles?

How do I see the relationship between PBLonline and the rest of the
curriculum?

What is the nature of the problem scenarios used in problem-based learning and assumptions implicit within the construction of these scenarios?

What do I see as the relationship between PBLonline and the assessment
methods?

How have I/will I create space that enables students to reflect upon
individual and collective goals?

Facilitation or moderation?

In earlier texts the notion of facilitation at different levels has been discussed
and in particular what might count as effective facilitation. Salmon has
provided a comprehensive guide to 'e-moderating.' An electronic moderator
is someone who 'presides over an electronic online meeting or conference'
(Salmon 2000: 3). She draws on research from staff and students' perspectives, offers guidance on training e-moderators and suggests a useful model
for teaching through computer mediated communication (CMC). Further,
Carlson provides a straightforward definition of a moderator online as one
whom:

helps people get started, gives them feedback, summarizes, weaves the
contributions of different folks together, gets it unstuck when necessary,
deals with individuals who are disruptive, or get off the track, brings in
new material to freshen it up periodically, and gets feedback from the

group on how things are going and what might happen from the group
on how things are going and what might happen next . . . [Further the
moderator needs to] communicate with the group as a whole, sub-groups,
and individuals to encourage participation.

(Carlson, 1989: 6.11)

However, there has been little documented in the literature about the role
of the facilitator in PBLonline. For some, there is an assumption that when
eight students share a computer to engage with a scenario, that it is sufficient
for a roving tutor to call round briefly to each team. Yet this does not mirror
the current notions of PBLonline facilitation, and in many ways downgrades
the role of the facilitator in a PBLonline team. A virtual model of facilitation
that reflects some of the best face-to-face problem-based learning facilitation
practices is required. Here, for example a facilitator could join in the email
debates students are having and call in on discussions. Yet there are problems
too with this in terms of staff time and students' participation. For example,
how do we deal with students who do not participate in PBLonline? How do
we deal with colleagues who are too directive and interfere with the team
process and progress?

In recent years there have been increasing debates about whether facilitation is just a form of good teaching or whether in fact it is something else
(for example, Boud and Miller, 1996). Such philosophizing has, until
recently, resulted in research being undertaken into the face-to-face facilitator
role with relatively little real exploration of what is meant by facilitation,
facilitator or the role of the facilitator by either researchers or participants in
the research. This confusion is not only seen in the research but also in the
way staff are equipped for implementing problem-based learning. For
example, many staff undergo facilitator training programmes but as yet there
seems to be little distinction made between the different but overlapping
roles. One way of engaging with this difficulty would be to argue for role
distinctions such as team facilitator, problem-based learning tutor and
programme manager. Equipping someone to facilitate a problem-based
learning team (a team facilitator) is a task that requires fewer capabilities than
the role of both facilitating a team while also designing materials and other
problem-based learning components of the curriculum (a problem-based
learning tutor). A further role might be that of problem-based learning programme manager, who designs the programme and oversees the implementation of problem-based learning, but may or may not be a problem-based
learning tutor or team facilitator as well. Although these roles do, to a large
extent, overlap, the distinction is important when undertaking research into
what might count as effective facilitation. Early work on exploration of the
role of different staff was identified by Peters (1998) who identified five types
of course design teams for distance learning, which are summarized below:

Type 1:   A university lecturer who is solely responsible for developing and running an online course. They may have had some experience of online learning but may not have worked as part of a team or know the literature on online education.

Type 2:   A university lecturer who co-authors with educational technologists.

Type 3:   A learning technologist or a group of learning technologists who are responsible for developing a course.

Type 4:   University lecturers, learning technologists, graphic designers, editors and media specialists who work together as a course team and develop a course for which they are jointly responsible.

Type 5:   An expert online teacher and experienced faculty member who is aware of the educational and technical issues of online learning and uses the support of a learning technologist for preparation of course materials.

These are the delineations of the kinds of types that are often seen in the design of PBLonline programmes. What tends to happen most often is the education drive for developing PBLonline comes from the Type 1 facilitators, who then seek support from one another and maybe also a learning technologist. The module or course is thus pedagogically driven but the materials are not always well designed in terms of learning technology. This then introduces issues as to what counts not just as good design but also good facilitation.

The 'good' facilitator in PBLonline

The difficulty with the whole notion of effectiveness in facilitation is that there is an implicit assumption that there are necessarily both right and better ways of facilitating PBLonline teams. While we can look to models of facilitation and question whether our role is that of a teacher, a tutor or a facilitator and seek to define those roles, these models and arguments do not really move us along in terms of equipping us to enable students to learn through problem-based learning. What I mean is that there appears to be an assumption that there are specific roles, attributes and ways of being that characterize some facilitation as 'good' or 'better' than other facilitation. Although it is inadvisable that the facilitator brings his own learning needs to the team discussion or attempts to create a culture of dependency in the team, to deny the inter-subjectivity of team and facilitator is somewhat naive.

Facilitators and students influence one another in a whole variety of ways, such as their views about what counts as knowledge, the interplay of content and process and the ways in which they do and do not deal with conflict in the team. Facilitators and PBLonline teams tend to shape and challenge each other, so that while most teams will meet the learning objectives of the programme or module as a minimum, they will do so in different ways because of team dynamics and the facilitator's pedagogical stance and academic positioning. Facilitation in PBLonline demands not just awareness but a personal transitional process, whereby we deeply critique the behaviours and actions we take up in the process of facilitating a PBLonline team. Many facilitators seem to oscillate between being directive towards students and saying very little at all. For example, many of them feel that in order for students to be competent and safe practitioners they need to direct them towards the right information so that they cover the material the facilitators expect. Alternatively, facilitators new to PBLonline often feel it is better to say less (or even nothing); so that the students feel that they are taking the lead in the learning. The first creates student dependency, the latter, particularly with students new to problem-based learning, results in students feeling that the lack of direction is duplicitous because they feel it is the facilitator's way of avoiding a declaration of their own agenda and concerns. Thus there needs to be a balance between these issues, so that the facilitator can be part of the team discussion in ways that the students themselves value. Not engaging in debate can be taken, by some students, as dis-interestedness or a belief that the facilitator is not prepared to express their own opinion and thus remain a voiceless participant. Finding this balance is difficult. Heron's model is useful here. Heron (1989, 1993) has suggested three modes of facilitation that are useful for helping novice facilitators to consider how they operate. They are as follows:

The hierarchical mode: The facilitators direct the learning process and exercise their power over it. Thus they decide (however covertly) the objectives of the team, challenge resistances, manage team feelings and provide structures for learning. In short, the facilitators take responsibility for the learning that takes place.

The co-operative mode: The facilitators share their power over the learning with the team and enable the team to become more self-directed by conferring with them. The facilitators prompt the team members to decide how they are going to learn and to manage confrontation. Although the facilitators share their own views, they are not seen as final but as one view amongst many.

The autonomous mode: The facilitators respect the total autonomy of the team; do not do things for the students or with them but give them the space and freedom to do things their own way. Without guidance, reminders or assistance, the team evolves its learning and structure, finds its own ways to manage conflict and gives meaning to personal and team learning. The facilitator's role is that of creating conditions in which students can exercise self-determination in their learning.

Although these delineations provided by Heron are useful to consider, there remain issues about how it is that staff are equipped to facilitate PBLonline.

Facilitating PBLonline in practice

Programmes where PBLonline has been successfully implemented and maintained over time invariably have been the ones where time and adequate resources have been spent in equipping staff from the outset. It is therefore important to plan the introduction of problem-based learning into the curriculum 1 or 2 years before the whole curriculum is changed. This will allow sufficient time to decide on the kind of programme that is to be designed and to prepare tutors adequately for the introduction of this new approach. A more detailed example of initial preparation of facilitators is presented in Murray and Savin-Baden (2000). The recommendations for educational development of staff are that:

1   The preparation for facilitators needs to start as early as possible, at least one year in advance of the commencement of the programme in which PBLonline is to be used. Many scholars now perceive the area of tutor development to be key to the success of problem-based learning and the number of tutor development workshops documented in recent years demonstrates this fact (for example, Almy *et al.*, 1992; Holmes and Kaufman, 1994; Little, 1997; Wilkerson and Hundert, 1997; Musal *et al.*, 2002; Zimitat and Miflin, 2003).
2   The development of scenarios should involve all groups of staff contributing to the delivery of a particular module.
3   The production of learning resources is vital to the success of PBLonline and related departments need to be involved from the outset.
4   In depth discussion about assessment values and methods should be a key component of any staff development programme.

It is important to equip staff by:

•   Providing educational development that will enable staff to become confident PBLonline facilitators, such as a specifically designed course.
•   Encouraging staff to work with learning technologists to develop appropriate online learning materials.
•   Helping staff to develop structured sessions such as team activities, booked chat sessions and to provide reading lists that make clear to the students that facilitation is about supporting and guiding rather than directing.
•   Ensuring staff understand that the pace of learning can be very different in PBLonline – such as fast busy discussion boards and frenetic chat sessions some weeks and slow ponderous posting with considerable reflection and silence other weeks.

Thus the following principles are worth considering:

Principles in PBLonline facilitation

Although it is possible to plan the programme well in advance and for staff members to undertake an e-moderation programme, there are some principles of facilitating PBLonline that differ from other models of e-moderation, in which facilitators should:

1   *Guide but not interrupt.* There is a tendency, particularly at the start of a session where students are presented with a new problem or activity, to interrupt or even pre-intervene by asking leading questions before the team have had a chance to discuss the problem. For example, if there is silence some staff will begin the scenario for the students by asking a question. It is better to wait, or to ask a gentle question such as 'what are the team thinking about this?

2   *Represent etiquette.* Although much has been written on online etiquette (netiquette) there are differences in PBLonline, particularly in relation to respecting silence, promoting student autonomy, and not interrupting when flaming occurs. This is largely because if facilitators interrupt or take control the locus of control shifts to the member of staff and the team does not deal with the problem or conflict themselves. There is a delicate balance here, but it is important for staff to model this and also to help students develop their own ground rules for their team.

3   *Acknowledge and use prior experience.* Many tutors feel that becoming a facilitator seems to be such a different role when they first begin that often they forget to draw on their prior experience. It is important to draw on earlier experiences, for example, one approach might be to reflect on the experience of being supervised in a research project. Often the supervisor guides the students in the early stages of the project, but towards the end the students may overtake their knowledge base. Another option might be to imagine the facilitator role as being that of a non-directive counsellor who uses reflection and questioning rather than direction.

4   *Recognize that being a facilitator means also being a learner.* This might mean learning to develop the capabilities of a facilitator and learning new knowledge with and through the students. The process of becoming a facilitator also demands developing and understanding the way in which facilitator and team influence one another in the learning process.

5   *Ensure that the team's concerns are heard.* Active listening skills are a prerequisite to good communication and are one of the most effective tools for helping online teams manage conflict. There is often an assumption that 'hearing' what is occurring online is very difficult, but learning to read the subtext of discussion forums and chat sessions is a skill facilitators need to

develop. Although this is complex to begin with, the ability to read team interactions in online spaces does develop over time.

6   *Listen and lurk positively.* There is often a tendency, after using straight forward online learning, to retain control rather than granting it to the students. The notion of 'lurking' often seems to imply that silence and watching are inherently bad, but students often need to watch and listen in PBLonline, so it is important not to confuse lurking with thinking space.

7   *Provide supportive interventions.* It is often easy to assume that not intervening means maintaining silence, but it is useful if students 'know' you are part of the discussion. Rather than just lurking it is helpful to students if the facilitators add some remark that illustrates they are listening and supporting the learning, but in a way that does not interrupt the students' discussion. Although this is difficult, statements such as 'I think this an interesting discussion' or 'would all the team agree with this?' are useful general statements for supporting students.

8   *Promote personal reflection.* Rather than weaving and summarizing the discussion as a facilitator, it is possible to encourage the students to reflect and summarize their own discussion and stances at the end of a given time period or problem. This encourages not only group reflection but also the synthesis of the process of what has occurred, as well as the synthesis of the information that has been collected and collated.

9   *Encourage team criticality.* One of the most difficult capabilities for students in PBLonline is in taking a critical stance. Many of those who have researched PBLonline report that there is a tendency for students to focus on the process of learning and the information collected, rather than taking a critical stance towards the way they are working and the knowledge produced (see for example Hmelo-Silver *et al.*, 2006; Lycke *et al.*, 2006). Ways of encouraging the development of criticality include the use of a team wiki, using blogs for assessment and asking students to summarize and critique each others' contributions. The latter activity is very demanding of students and often difficult to do, but if the teams have been well supported and are cohesive this is often a possibility. One way of beginning this process is to use interesting activities *within* the team which are competitive, such as treasure hunts, but where the team themselves have to decide which team member wins and say why this is.

10   *Use intuition.* In the context of PBLonline little attention has been given to the role of intuition in facilitation. Arguments abound as to whether uploading handouts and detailed lecture notes onto WebCT/Blackboard is something that helps or hinders student learning. Yet both staff and students' stories of their experience of PBLonline would seem to suggest that intuition

is very much part of the process of learning and facilitation. Facilitators often speak of knowing when the team is going well, but also of times when there were difficulties in the team, that they could neither define nor verbalize how they even knew were present.

However, it is important to note that there are also many difficulties in using PBLonline and Donnelly (2006: 96) has suggested that the following might occur in PBLonline:

- asking too many questions – balancing between those asked face-to-face and online;
- transferring your anxiety onto the student;
- finding a quick solution – only dealing with the presenting problem;
- feeling inadequate with the student;
- wanting to do everything for the student;
- blocking the student's emotions;
- wanting to be liked by the student;
- being too busy to listen;
- dictating and imposing your own values on the student;
- not being clear about what you can and cannot offer in the way of help (fuzzy boundaries).

The balance between freedoms and constraints, and technological and pedagogical elements is a constant challenge in PBLonline facilitation. However, as Collison *et al.* (2000) point out, there is a need to open up online spaces and provide freedom for students to 'hang out' in spaces which are not facilitated or 'policed' by teaching staff.

Preparing and equipping students for PBLonline

Although the research into the way in which students are prepared for PBLonline is sparse, this is a growing area of concern. There has been relatively little research that has explored students' experience of e-facilitation in the context of PBLonline. However, students' ability to be independent learners as opposed to dependent ones, was affected by their abilities to both engage with the dialectic between the prerequisites of the educational programme and use these prerequisites to support and enhance their own learning needs. Furthermore, it is vital that students develop not only as a team but also as an online community. Boettcher and Conrad (1999: 88) define an online learning community as a community that 'consists of learners who support and assist each other, make decisions synergistically, and communicate with peers on a variety of topics beyond those assigned'. Below are some of the strategies that will help to not only equip students, but also help them to become an online community in their PBLonline teams:

1   Ensure that students undertaking the course can use email, and have the right internet connection and a browser that fits with that of the university. For example, there have been compatibility problems between Internet Explorer and WebCT Vista.

2   Provide warm-up sessions in the first week of the course so that students become familiar with chat, discussion forums and the ability to read and write online – pointing out the spell checker in the discussion board is helpful as mis-spelling does upset some (often mature) students.

3   Encourage students to meet in chat sessions in the first 2 weeks of the course before they use chat for team sessions so that they are familiar with the medium.

4   Use activities and scenarios at the outset that build individual and team confidence.

5   Ensure students know what they are expected to do – a week by week schedule can be helpful for this, but also when and how. One useful approach is to provide pop-up windows at the start of each week that remind students of the activities for the week.

6   Provide students with resources that support them which are both located online and sent to them as hard copies. Students new to PBLonline often forget passwords, how to access different areas and spaces and misunderstand their role, that of the team and the instructions given to them. Step by step guides are a vital support, particularly if they include graphics, diagrams and web shots to illustrate how things appear and operate.

7   Ensure students realize they can email tutors to communicate concerns and difficulties. Many students are afraid of doing this, but one to one support can be vital at the start of a PBLonline module.

8   Ensure students understand that they have choice over the direction of their learning and that it is their responsibility to collaborate and co-operate with others.

9   Explain what collaboration means in PBLonline, such as questioning each other, sharing resources, co-operating rather than competing, learning to value teamwork, accepting diverse perspectives and enjoying the possibility of disagreement and conflict as a means to team and individual learning.

10   Provide opportunities to discuss:

- Student disjunction – getting stuck, feeling frustrated and fragmented.
- Notions of lurking in teams.
- Silence and humour.
- Over engagement in the learning.

The following case study provides a reflection on a number of the issues presented above:

Case study

This case study presents perspectives of two students, who were also academics, involved on an online programme, that while not delineated as a PBLonline programme contained many features of a distance PBLonline approach. The case explores the underlying reasons for undertaking this course, how the students experienced 'stuckness', and the particular catalysts that caused this disjunction.

The stories

Clare was an academic, who had two motivations for undertaking the programme: one an awareness that she needed to redress the fact that she was slipping behind in her understanding of the 'e' environment and the other, the main one, to experience actually being an e-learning student.

Anna, while enjoying the general shift to e-learning in higher education, was constantly frustrated by what she saw as the 'clunkiness' of learning in online spaces. She decided that the best way to prevent any further courses she developed from being completely vanilla was to become a learner for her 'self'.

Silence and stuckness

The overarching sense of silence and stuckness pervaded the course for both students. For example, not only lurking on the discussion boards, but not knowing what they thought, how to position themselves, what to say. While stuckness was largely characterized by conflict, ambiguity and incoherence, sometimes it seemed as if they were just pedagogically immobile; at other times they were cross and frustrated, knowing there must be better ways of attempting tasks but not really knowing where to start. The notion of what presence and embodiment meant in digital spaces was something that was constantly problematic for both students. The way they seemed to cope in this silent space in the earlier stages of the course was to (super) impose what they 'knew' using an identity they felt they 'had'. Clare and Anna both intuitively felt that this new learning space was distinctively different, but also argued that it might be that they were imposing difference on it because it was new and unfamiliar, which would seem to be a contestable position, just as is the notion that they were somehow disembodied in cyberspace. Yet at the same time ordering proved to be a source of discomfort for both students.

Catalysts to silence and stuckness

Clare and Anna found becoming stuck in learning was both deeply problematic and useful and transformative. This is echoed in the similarities in their experience and also in the differences in their responses. However, there were trends they shared and in particular they both felt that their stuckness did not necessarily *always* result in the displacement of their identity (in the sense of a shift causing such a sense of disjunction that it resulted in costs personally and pedagogically, and hence had a life cost) but rather a shift in their identity or role perception so that issues and concerns were seen and heard in new and different ways.

Technical difficulties and understandings

Both students, despite being familiar with VLEs, found that the volume of links, information, reading and in particular the speed of communication and learning made them feel awash with complexity. This was partly as a result of the sheer enthusiasm of their cohort who posted daily (and more) to the discussion board, but it was also because others had so much really useful knowledge (and links) to share. While both students enjoyed the stimulation, there were times when they fell silent because of feeling overwhelmed and almost voiceless in the discussion spaces.

Feeling out of control

There were more fascinating leads to follow up than there was time available – an inevitable outcome of such a widely experienced group of staff and students. Feelings of being out of control would arise when the students were not able to access the site for a while, or could not keep up with tasks because of other work and commitments. In such circumstances they used strategies to regain control by focusing on essential tasks, such as blogging and completing assignments. There was a sense at times of over engaging with activities that seemed safe and familiar, or in Anna's case new and quirky (such as Second Life), and at other times a sense of avoidance characterized by feelings of being overwhelmed and stuck by the discussion, activities and readings.

It was possible to locate Clare and Anna's different forms of disjunctions and silences in the following two ways:

1   A moment of conceptual puzzlement: here self-realization that they were stuck and did not understand how to move on resulted in a sense of feeling paralysed or fragmented.
2   A cycle of stuckness: here they understood the need to move away from a particular position of stuckness, but not knowing how or where to move resulted in a constant cycle of stuckness which led to a return to the same stuck space repeatedly. When this occurred they tended to opt for silence or actually became silent by being in this cycle.

Conclusions

The students' experience here was liminal, a betwixt and between state but the boundaries, edges and thresholds they encountered were sometimes similar and sometimes different. When the students became stuck they reacted to the silence in two distinctive ways – by avoiding or over-engaging. Such avoidance and over-engagement might be seen as manifestations of 'lurking'. This is perhaps an extended definition, emphasizing the 'prowling' aspect of lurking as well as the 'not responding' aspect.

Conclusion

Effective facilitation demands not only that we acknowledge and manage diversity but also that we learn to trust the judgements and intuitions of ourselves, our colleagues and our students. For example, in many ways, it is easier to avoid engagement with complex issues that are perhaps seen as being disruptive; than it is to help students learn to manage the issues within their team. Facilitators need to be aware of such complexities so that that they do not silence some and privilege others. Development of PBLonline facilitation is still at a comparatively early stage and, as in any new venture, will require time and practise by tutors to develop new skills related not only to manipulating the technological tools, but also to developing appropriate user-friendly content and feedback for students. However, the way in which our PBLonline courses are designed and implemented will also affect the kinds of facilitation that are possible in PBLonline and it is to this that we turn in Chapter 5.

Part 2

Designing problem-based learning online environments

Design choices

Introduction

This chapter will raise questions for the reader relating to design choices regarding PBLonline and offer the reader ways of making informed design decisions. It begins by exploring some of the issues that need to be considered when designing PBLonline, from a technological perspective rather than a pedagogical one. By starting with what it is we want students to learn, it is argued that we can focus on the students' experience rather than the notion of content coverage. It is important too to move away from the idea of PBLonline being a course that uses knowledge repository. Instead this chapter will suggest, by using a design scheme that focuses on learning intentions, assessment and the development of capability, that the kinds of PBLonline on offer can focus on liquid learning and the ability of students to develop judgments, criticality and the ability to interrogate texts.

Chapter 5 begins by suggesting a schema for the development of PBL-online, and then gives an overview of a possible PBLonline module that provides learning intentions, and suggests activities and resources. The last section of the chapter illustrates activities that may be used in PBLonline programmes, such as simulations, web quests and games.

So where do you start? A PBLonline course design schema

This section offers a flexible schema that can be used for modules, units and whole programmes. It reflects the philosophy of PBLonline being an approach that is a student-centred philosophy and thus allows for students to negotiate and/or include their own aims:

1   Consider what it is you want students to learn – not what content you want them to cover.
2   Decide how this learning will be assessed.
3   Make a list of what you want them to learn (your learning intentions).

4   Break down your learning intentions into a list of capabilities, know-ledges, understandings.
5   Decide how you expect them to learn.
6   Locate ways of enabling them to illustrate what they have learnt, this may be thought of in terms of assessment or in other ways.
7   Provide learning intentions that allow students to show that they are working towards a particular capability, even if they have not yet attained it.
8   Provide learning intentions that show how students may have moved beyond the intentions specified.

Considerable time and effort must go into the preparation and design of both programmes and online materials, but in the context of problem-based learning there needs to be a real clarity about how the course and the scenarios are created, so that they produce robust educational discussion. The exemplar illustrates how the schema might be put into practice and then used to develop a complete overview as in Table 2.3.

The schema for a module in learning and teaching in online spaces may thus be designed as shown in Table 5.1 This schema is useful for the initial design of the course and shifts the focus away from learning through behavioural objectives. Instead, the focus is on the *intentions* of learning. This is important because problem-based learning and PBLonline are not approaches to learning that sit well with outcome-focused behavioural objectives. Using learning intentions is based on both Stenhouse (1975) and Pratt *et al.* (1998), combining Stenhouse's notion of 'induction' and Pratt's notion of 'Social reform.' For Stenhouse, induction involves the introduction of someone into the thought system of the culture and here successful induction would be characterized by a person's ability to develop relation-ships and judgments in relation to that culture – induction. For some people it would also be seen as education – in its broadest sense. Pratt has suggested that social reform is a perspective of education, whereby effective teaching seeks to change society in substantive ways:

> Teachers in this perspective are concerned with changing the social norms of society or a profession. From this perspective, effective teachers awaken students to values and ideologies that are embedded in texts and common practices within their discipline or profession . . . To do so, teachers help learners analyze and deconstruct common practices for ways in which such practices perpetuate conditions that are unacceptable. Texts are interrogated for what is said and what is not said; what is included and what is excluded; who is represented and who is omitted from the dominant discourse.
>
> (Pratt and Collins, 2006)

Table 5.1 Schema for PBLonline module in learning and teaching, undergraduate, third year

Steps of schema	Example
1 Consider what it is you want students to learn	• Theories of adult learning • Ability to critique literature • Understanding of value of different theorist work to different contexts • Be able to discuss theories as a PBL team in a discussion forum
2 Decide how learning will be assessed	• Team Wiki • Individual blog
3 Make a list of what you want them to learn (your learning intentions)	• To be able to analyse adult learning theory • To be able to appraise the values underpinning different teaching and learning theories • To be able to evaluate a range of technologies in terms of their impact on teaching and learning
4 Break down of learning intentions into a list of capabilities, knowledges, understandings	• To know how to design own (online) learning resources • To understand own practice in terms of the issues emerging from research in learning and teaching • To know the role of the teacher in different learning contexts • To understand how to evaluate teaching and learning strategies in action • To be able to identify principles of assessment and discuss their application to a number of situations • To identify their learner stance and those of others
5 Decide how you expect them to learn, i.e. what learning activities will they undertake	• Annotate the key features of a research paper and upload individual perspectives onto team writeboard • Browsing texts to identify key features and critique them • Discuss texts in team in discussion forum
6 Locate ways of enabling them to illustrate what they have learnt	• They are able to analyse a range of texts and discuss them in the discussion forum • They are able to delineate difference between learning and teaching theorists and apply this to the scenario they are working on
7 Learning intentions that allow students to show they are working towards a capability	• They are able to suggest if the theoretical claims are justified and underpinned by sound research practice and identify key features of each
8 Provide learning intentions that show how students may have moved beyond the intentions specified	• They are able to sort range theorists into research-led and theoretical conceptions of teaching and learning and list the reasons for their choices through direct reference to the texts

Learning intentions thus focus on what is being learned; on what the teacher intends rather than what the teacher *wants* the outcome of the learning to be. Using learning intentions mirrors the values and philosophy of problem-based learning and reflects the argument that it is learner-centred rather than teacher-centred. However, the types of problem scenarios that need to be created to reflect an intentional model of curriculum design are often ill-structured and are ones that engage students in moral dilemmas. For example, Schmidt and Moust (2000a) have explicated different problem types, but also suggest that the way in which questions are asked of students tends to guide the types of knowledge in which students engage; problem types will be explored in more depth in Chapter 4. Ill-structured problems are important in PBLonline because they help students to engage in complex issues, introduce challenges and promote team discussion. Also, with the shift towards the use of open source software and Web 2.0 technologies, the ability to move across different online environments is constantly changing. However, in terms of examining the pedagogy of PBLonline perhaps it is also advantageous to look at designing the pedagogy as well as the structure.

What might it look like?

There follows a model of a PBLonline programme for a team of four to six students engaging in a scenario that takes place over anything from 1 to 6 weeks. However, three important principles here are that:

1   Staff involved in the module should design the scenarios, and these should be constantly online so that the students can see what is planned for the module as a whole. (It is also very useful to leave scenarios and discussion threads up for several months after modules have finished, so that students can return to them, examine them, and use the information for future scenarios and assessments.)
2   Resources should be wide ranging and comprehensive (such as readings, podcasts, websites) so that students are not directed towards particular material and instead develop their own list of learning needs.
3   Students should be encouraged to read and think through the scenario before coming online, so that as individuals they have considered their own learning needs.

The module design (see Table 5.2) is based on a module for students to learn about teaching and learning theories at Master's level. It is undertaken through the virtual 3D world Second Life and utilizes games and webquests as well as problem-based learning scenarios. In practice over a three-week period, this might be undertaken as follows:

Session 1: Warm-up session. In the first session of PBLonline it is useful for students to use the time as a warm-up for the rest of the module. This will enable them to become familiar with the learning environment being used,

Table 5.2 Overview of a PBLonline module

Session	Time on task	Learning intention	Activity	Location	Resources	Role of e-facilitator
1	2 or 3 postings	Be able to discuss warm-up scenarios	Warm-up problem in allotted groups	Discussion board	Students' prior experience	Provide support, answers initial concerns
2	60–90 mins + postings	Be able to define team learning needs	Scenario 1	Discussion in teams MSN chat × 1	Students' experience Readings	Facilitate understanding of scenarios
3	60 mins × 2	Share research Synthesize findings	Scenario 1 (continued) Second Life orientation activity	MSN chat × 2	Students' experience Second Life instructions and guidance	Facilitate process
4	2 or 3 postings	Be able to walk and fly in Second Life	Scenario 2	Discussion	Readings	Facilitate understanding of scenarios
5		Be able to define team learning needs	Scenario 2 (continued)	Chat sessions	Podcasts	Facilitate process
6	Self-directed time managed by teams and students	Share research Synthesize findings	Scenario 2 (continued)		Readings	Supporting and responding
7		Understand learning in Second Life	Scenario 3		Second Life Readings	Supporting students working as an effective team
8	Each session should take a student	Be able to work as a team in Second Life	Scenario 3 (continued)	Second Life		Encouraging students to critique each others' work and stance
9	2 hours, which includes time for team work	Understand how team learning operate in Second Life	Scenario 3 (continued)	Second Life		
10		Be able to work as a team to decide which online space to use	Scenario 4	Discussion board, writeboards, chat	Readings	Facilitate process
11		Understand each others' perspectives with regard to working in disembodied spaces	Scenario 4 (continued)	Discussion board or Second Life		Encouraging students to critique each other's work and stance
12		Evaluate the value of learning in diverse online spaces	Synthesis of group interaction	Write boards		Facilitate team critique and reflection

meet one another and ask questions about the module of each other and the facilitator. Note, that as with most online learning, it is useful to ask students to start the discussion by introducing themselves before asking the team to work on one of the PBLonline scenarios. Warming up and helping students to feel confident is particularly important in PBLonline, as students easily become distressed about working on a scenario without first feeling they have had some time to get to know each other as a team, and become familiar with the particular quirks of the virtual learning environment being used to support the module. However, there is often a tendency by the facilitator to over scaffold the learning through a strong e-moderating presence that can hinder the development of team autonomy.

Box 5.1 Warm-up scenario for Session 1

The invisible student

Quite a kind of pleasing, liberating moment almost, was towards the end of the programme. We had little clips, kind of resumes that you could send to each other, where you presented the kind of identity you wanted to present to the world, and it didn't have a picture facility in those days, but people just wrote a little cameo of themselves.

And there was a woman in Australia who'd given hers, and towards the end I said something about – there was something happening in Australia where she lived – and I said, 'Are you going to kind of go along and take part in that?', and she said 'Well no I can't because I'm a wheelchair user'.

And that was right towards the end of the course and she had chosen to disclose that at that point. And that was interesting 'cos there was no way in that environment that that had appeared at all before. And I'm sure had we known that from the outset, if it was in a face-to-face environment, it'd have been the usual thing, you would have probably treated her quite differently in that sense.

And I realized that that was quite a valuable aspect of this kind of environment, that it gives the users of it a certain control over what they disclose about their identities. By that point we'd all worked together and it was irrelevant really at that point. And the identity had already been constructed I think for her as a member of the group, and I looked at her as a learner and a group member, rather than as a person with a disability. So that was quite nice.

A useful warm-up activity is to provide student teams with different scenarios that relate to them, such as from an online learning situation. The idea is that at the end of Session 1 teams come together as a cohort on the discussion board to share their learning experiences and their findings. This will work well with an overall cohort of 30 students or less, but larger cohorts will need to be divided into groups of around 30. Two such examples (see Boxes 5.1 and 5.2) have been provided by Sian Bayne at The University of Edinburgh. Students are asked to consider the key issues around the behaviours and communicative features of working in online learning groups

---

Box 5.2 Warm-up scenario for Session 1

The saboteur

Actually it was this year, one very vocal and rather disaffected student who had taken against the university as a whole but then took against this module in particular, claiming that in doing the module online we were trying to do education on the cheap, and that it was an attempt to monitor – sort of Big Brother style – students and their learning processes, and that what we were trying to teach was banal and beneath his notice.

And his arrogance coloured the way the students reacted to the whole module. I had to point out to him that in fact the system was not trying to do education on the cheap and that it was costing the university rather more than it would do with traditional methods, and that in no way were we trying to use it as a way of monitoring students because that would be illegal. And that shut him up on that, but what he subsequently went on to do was to start attacking students online for their views.

He's a student who has difficulties at home I suppose and he's very opinionated, particularly about music and politics and the like. He caused quite a lot of disruption and had to be seen by his head of department twice. He tried to encourage students to post loads and loads of messages to flood the system and crash it, and that was clearly not in the spirit of the thing!

He then posted a message that talked about how to use drugs safely which I immediately withdrew from the system; hoping no-one else had seen it. So I took it off because it was in a sense promoting drugs, and again I felt that that was not what the system was there for. He upset a lot of students with his arrogant approaches to their comments.

and post a message to the discussion board describing how they would deal with the situation.

These scenarios introduce issues about etiquette, and as well as an etiquette guide being included in the course handbook, it is important that students discuss this in-depth at the outset. This is because although many students will be familiar with some forms of online learning, in PBLonline teams require patience, honesty and cooperation to work effectively. Furthermore, communicating through avatars in 3D worlds also introduces challenges about embodiment and what is, and is not, deemed as acceptable behaviour. For example, it is important to use the person's avatar name rather than their 'real' name, and jumping is often used as a greeting whereas bumping someone else is considered rude and unacceptable practice.

Session 2. The team meets with the facilitator for a 'private chat,' in short a facilitated online problem-based learning seminar. Scenario 1 may be discussed for about 60–90 minutes, during which the tutor helps students to define their learning needs, while also checking understanding and ensuring that students have shared out tasks fairly around the team. However, the skill required of the tutor in this session is in not intervening too soon, thereby enabling students to make their own decisions about their particular learning needs.

In cases where students are new to undertaking problem-based learning or even PBLonline, it is advisable that students are encouraged to use a shared writeboard during meetings, so that they can reflect on their progress in preparation for the next tutorial.

Before Session 3 students are expected to upload their own material from their tasks and experience, to share with the rest of the team. This needs to be done a day or two prior to this meeting, so that all students have time to read the materials and tutors can examine what has been uploaded.

Session 3, part 1: Discussion and co-construction. At a prescribed time the team holds the first meeting of Session 3 with the tutor, and having read the materials that have been uploaded, they debate and ask questions of each other and seek clarification on materials not understood. The latter part of this meeting is spent working out how to apply this material to Scenario 1, and to check whether there have been any omissions in the researched materials that need to be addressed. Between this meeting and the next, students will be expected to work asynchronously or in scheduled discussion (decided by them) in order to apply the researched material. The next meeting is a discussion between students of what has been presented, and students reflect on the process. This 'meeting' can be synchronous or asynchronous.

Session 3, part 2: Second Life introduction. The second component of Session 3 is a Second Life orientation activity in which students are given instructions for downloading the Second Life software. They are expected to create and dress an avatar and meet in Second Life at a given coordinate.

Sessions 4, 5 and *6* are repeated as above, using Scenario 2, but with greater complexity as students become more familiar with the process.

Sessions 7, 8 and *9.* These sessions are problem-based learning seminars held in Second Life in spaces such as that shown in Figure 5.1.

Students begin Session 7 by meeting together, learning to fly and changing clothes. The Second Life scenario may occur as a traditional scenario in a screen in-world, but is more likely to be a game or a Second Life quest.

Sessions 10, 11. These sessions can either be based in Second Life or in the online teams via chat sessions and the discussion board, the decision being made by each team individually.

Session 12. This session is designed for each team of students to share their perspectives on (or 'solution' to) each of the scenarios across the cohort, using a shared writeboard. This offers a space for discussion, argument and the exploration of different approaches taken.

Figure 5.1 Learning space in Second Life

PBLonline activities

One of the issues that it is important to consider in PBLonline is that of ensuring that there are a variety of activities, so that students sustain interest across the module. This section suggests some possible problem-based learning activities that might be used in PBLonline. These activities are similar to e-tivities (Salmon, 2002) in that they are designed to motivate learning. However, they are not only based in interaction through message contributions nor are they always necessarily asynchronous. PBLonline activities are designed to enable students to develop a stance toward the knowledge and queries in which they are engaging and to challenge them to develop independence in inquiry. Thus activities here are not usually bite-size but are complex and messy, and so do not always have clear goals or outcomes. Instead they are designed to stimulate discussion and questions between members of the cohorts and can include any or all of the following:

Simulations

Simulations have been used in conjunction with problem-based learning for many years, but largely as a component of face-to-face programmes. For example, Rendas *et al.* (1999) introduced a computer simulation that was designed for problem-based learning in order to motivate learning, structure knowledge in a clinical context and develop learning skills for medical students at a stage in the programme when they had had little contact with patients. It was also designed to evaluate how students reasoned and learned in each session. The problem situation provided all the information about a patient in a predetermined sequence and students, working three to a computer, were expected to find out further information by asking one question at a time, seeking justification for the hypothesis they had put forward and being encouraged to identify learning issues. The answers provided by the students were logged and later analysed with a tutor. The difficulty with this particular model of computer simulation is that it offers students little opportunity for creativity and personal responsibility and in many ways resembles some of the earlier forms of guided discovery. What is really occurring here is that problem-solving learning is being used to guide students to the right answer or diagnosis.

An example of this would be the virtual autopsy developed by the University of Leicester Medical School, UK. This effective tool has proved to be a useful way of learning for students. However, it is essentially diagnostic in nature and thus students follow a step-by-step approach to solving a problem that encourages reductionist rather than constructivist forms of learning. This is fine if it is presented as problem-solving learning and it is acknowledged that problem situations have just been designed around particular disciplines or diseases. Yet in many cases it is referred to as computer aided or computer simulated problem-based learning, which causes confusions for staff, students and those seeking to imitate this approach in other disciplines or institutions. However, there are other simulations developed within universities that have not been developed for PBLonline but could easily be adapted for it. For example, Aisling is a virtual town at the University of Hull, UK, which focuses on people and their lives and is used in blended health care modules, but could easily be adopted for PBLonline.

Off-the-shelf simulations?

An important advantage of problem-based learning is the way in which it promotes dialogic learning and thus such an advantage is lost when staff or students work alone at a computer and do not discuss the scenario with peers. It may seem that the use of computer simulation is ill advised, but in fact, this is not the case. All problem scenarios in problem-based learning curricula need to be well designed and tested before use and it is the same with computer simulations. In some cases, a computer simulation may be better used as a component of a scenario, rather than the scenario itself. Simulations need to be located within problem-based learning rather than used as a mechanism or strategy to try to promote problem-based learning.

Web quests

The original idea of WebQuests dates back to the relatively early days of the World Wide Web and are a form of treasure hunt conducted in the arena of the Web. The resources may be Web documents, but they may also include human sources and experts who can be accessed via networked communication channels such as email. WebQuests may be relatively simple tasks involving searching for information, or they can be complex and staged activities that extend over long periods of time, such as Alternative Reality Games. Web quests, then may be seen as a research activity in which students collect and analyse information using the Web, which in many ways mirrors the processes involved in problem-based learning. Webquests were invented by Bernie Dodge and Tom March at San Diego State University in 1995, and a particularly useful tool that can be used to develop webquests in a short space of time is InstantWebquest which is a web-based software.

Treasure hunts

Online treasure hunts can be done in a variety of ways and can be designed either by the tutor or by the students themselves (by an opposing PBLonline team). The treasure hunt can take the form of a cryptic treasure hunt on the web, or be more inventive through using Google Earth or Multi-User Virtual

Environments (MUVEs) such as Second Life, whereby students are asked to find a series of objects or buy and sell objects.

Games

There is increasing interest in the use of problem-based learning games since part of the skill of a game in this context is in the skill of learning to learn. Further, making collaborative decisions as a team is an important goal; however, it is vital that the characters within the game are people with whom the students can identify. Games, to a large extent, do mirror many of the complexities inherent in problem-based learning, such as uncertainty and exploration. In the context of discussing games Kane has argued:

> Play is about freedom. But is also about the freedom to get it wrong. Not only do we play, but we are often played with – by others, by systems of which we are elements and by the sheer unpredictability, uncertainty and complexity of life.
>
> (Kane, 2005: 50)

Finally, just as dialogue is central to problem-based learning, so it is to online interactive games. For example, Ravenscroft and Matheson (2002) suggest the importance that dialogue facilitation games hold in improving students' conceptual understanding through dialogue rather than through competition. Examples of games that might be useful here are social impact games such as FoodForce, or the more recent Infiniteams which promotes team skills and leadership characteristics. These are discussed in more detail in Chapter 7.

Problems

The issue of what might count as a problem and the complexity of problem design is something that is a challenge to many tutors implementing problem-based learning, whether face-to-face or in online contexts. Some people design the problems themselves; others use templates or download problems that can be adapted. Heron (1993) proposed that teams engage in four types of task:

> *Renewal tasks*: such tasks involve using or updating equipment or undertaking education and training. Teams involved in such tasks include technical teams and staff development teams.
>
> *Development tasks*: here the work of the team is to innovate and work in new directions and often to solve or manage problems. A problem-based learning team would be one that is, in general, focused on development tasks.

Production tasks: the team's function here is to produce goods or services.

Crisis tasks: the team role is to deal with dangers, emergencies and critical events. Some problem-based learning teams (in areas such as health, social care and disaster management) may be involved in this area.

Heron has suggested that too much focus on one of these areas results in distortions within the team. Problems then emerge in the forms of teams becoming person bound, problem bound, role bound or power bound. His notion of teams becoming problem bound is particularly useful in the context of problem-based learning. Teams preoccupied with problem-solving work tend to become focused on goals, planning and achievement.

This leads to decision-making control becoming subservient to a pre-occupation with problem-solving tasks and the pursuit of technical know-how, and occurs at the expense of a coherent social structure, and of personnel welfare. The resources section at the end of the book illustrates a number of scenarios that work well online and will demonstrate the way in which links and supporting material are used to enhance team collaboration.

Chat

Online chat can refer to any kind of communication over the internet, but is primarily meant to refer to one to one chat or text-based group chat (formally also known as synchronous conferencing), using tools such as instant messaging applications. Live chat sessions are essential to PBLonline since in such sessions students develop capabilities for working effectively as an online team. Live chats are also often spaces used by students to summarize progress to date, synthesize information and decide how to progress as a team. To date, chat sessions seem to be somewhat underused in PBLonline, but it is a medium that has been used successfully by authors such as Lycke *et al.* (2006).

Discussion forums

These are important for holding discussions and posting user generated content. Discussion forums are also commonly referred to as web forums, message boards, discussion boards, (electronic) discussion groups and bulletin boards. While these are valuable places for PBLonline, they can be a burden if teams are too large or if team members over post or make elongated postings. While Salmon (2000), following Feenburg (1989) argues for weaving, the pulling together of participants' perspectives and relating them to the theory ideas in the course, this is not always useful in PBLonline. This is because if the facilitator rather than the students weaves (or perhaps just weaves too much) students will not weave within their team, which is important for the synthesis and co-construction of knowledge within the team. However, it is important that students are encouraged to keep contestation polite and to respond to others' contributions. Students should be encouraged to keep board postings reasonably short and to the point – especially as long, very intricate contributions tend to be ignored.

3D virtual worlds/multi-user virtual environments

Second Life is a 3D virtual world created by LindenLab set in an Internet-based world. Residents (in the forms of self-designed avatars) in this world interact with each other and can learn, socialize, participate in activities, and buy and sell items with one another, While Second Life remains very popular there are other MUVEs which offer opportunities to develop PBLonline such as Terra Nova, Entropia Universe, Dotsoul and possibly Cyberpark.

Readings

The readings provided for the course should be wide ranging in style and information, and should include websites, essays, newsletters and the like, as well as journal articles. In PBLonline students must not be guided or directed, but must instead use each other as sources, find their own materials and decide what is important for them to use. However, it is useful in the early stages to offer students materials that will support them until they become more familiar with the technology and the approach to learning.

Conclusion

The diversity and complexity of online and distance education means that it is not unproblematic to utilize PBLonline pedagogically in the curriculum and in higher education in general. However, by developing PBLonline through schema and using learning intentions rather than behavioural objectives, it becomes possible to design programmes that fit with both the technology and the pedagogy of this approach. The choices relating to ways in which design decisions are made in relation to PBLonline will be explored in Chapter 6. In particular this next chapter explores how first gaining understanding of the different constellations of PBLonline is vital in then deciding which type to adopt and how that will impact upon learning.

Deciding which form of PBLonline to adopt

Introduction

Online education continues to be a growth area in education but many of the frustrations in universities seem to stem from the expense of new equipment, the speed of change and the need for continual updating. Universities have tight budgets, and securing funds for new systems to support online learning seems to be a constant battleground. There continue to be debates too, about the form and content of online education, and this has been captured by Mason who has argued that: 'Many computer-based teaching programs whether stand alone, or on an Intranet or the Web, fall into one of two categories: all glitz and no substance, or content that reflects a rote-learning, right/wrong approach to learning' (Mason, 1998: 4).

In many curricula it could be argued that this is still very much the case. However, the more recent focus on students as customers and approaches such as problem-based learning have forced a reappraisal and a redesigning of online education, so that it can facilitate the development of knowledge management, problem-solving, critique and learning how to learn.

This chapter will explore the choices and decisions that need to be made when deciding which form of PBLonline to adopt. It will examine examples from around the world, in order to exemplify how different forms can work well, merely survive or fail. It will raise questions for the reader relating to design choices regarding PBLonline learning and offer the reader ways of making informed design decisions through the use of a series of steps. It will also explore the complexities of managing effective online collaboration and group dynamics and use mini case studies to illustrate success and failure from those experienced in this field.

The type of design adopted will relate not only to the country, university and discipline into which PBLonline is placed, but also to the type of PBLonline being adopted. There are, however, some general principles encapsulated in the following ten steps.

Ten steps to implementing PBLonline

This section suggests that it is important to consider the following ten steps when considering the implementation of PBLonline. By using these steps it will ensure that many of the common mistakes and assumptions are avoided and that the focus is on learning and collaboration rather than teaching and content coverage.

Step 1: Working with/in the virtual learning environment

Most universities already have some form of virtual learning environment in place, which offer varying degrees of flexibility. Although many proprietary VLEs such as WebCT/Blackboard remain somewhat conventional and tend to make learning linear and feel contained, many staff have used PBLonline within such software. What perhaps matters, in the context of traditional VLEs, is to design the problem-based learning in interesting and innovative ways, link it to other software that may be external to the VLE and create innovative approaches to assessment. For example, PebblePad is an e-Portfolio system that allows users to build and develop artefacts related to their studies.

Open source software does provide more flexibility and certainly the blog facilities in many proprietary VLEs are extremely basic. However, Moodle has become increasingly popular and Bodington also appears to be gaining some popularity. The recent development of Sloodle, a blending of Second Life and Moodle, allows students to post blog entries directly from Second Life and tags the entry with a Second Life weblink (SLURL), has also been welcomed. Further, Elgg spaces are increasingly being adopted, often in conjunction with a traditional VLE at several universities, because they are a centrally hosted service. These spaces can be accessed at any time of day with any web-enabled device, with any web browser and navigation in multiple languages.

Steps 2 and 3: Decide what you want students to learn and how you will assess this learning

These decisions are probably the most important ones to make at the beginning of course design. Although this might appear an obvious statement to suggest, too many staff begin course design with a focus on what content should be covered rather than what is to be learned and assessed. For example, Mason (1998) suggested three online course models that, although simple, offer an understanding of the varying ways different online communities engage with problem-based learning. In the *Content + Support model* course content is, in general, separate from tutorial support. Content is provided for the students either on the web or as a package of material, whereas tutorial support is given via email or computer conferencing and this support usually represents no more than 20 per cent of the students' study time. Thus in practice the online elements tend to be added on, and the course material is designed in ways that can be tutored by teachers other than those who have written the content.

The result of a Content + Support model then is the provision by staff of a 'knowledge repository'. The idea of a 'knowledge repository' is a term I use to reflect the idea that many programmes still use VLEs as places to deposit large amounts of 'knowledge' that students are supposed to cover. Students can then just access this knowledge, download it, file it and use it to pass their assignment. This merely reflects the idea that there is 'solid' knowledge to be covered. Solid knowledge is characterized by a notion that there are certain facts and things that must be known. Bauman (2000) suggested that in the age of solid modernity, before the 1960s, there was a sense that accidents and sudden or surprising events were seen as temporary irritants, since it was still possible to achieve a fully rational perfect world. Solid modernity was characterized by slow change, where structures were seen as being tough and unbreakable. Solid knowledge might therefore be seen as rational, tough and unbreakable. Thus, in this model, the notion of the development of an online community is severely restricted by the strong division between support and content. This means that students have no real sense of building up experience of working collaboratively online or supporting one another through online communication. Although the advantage of this model is that the high course development costs can be offset by low presentation costs, the actual possibility for collaborative working is limited. The result is that if this model is used for problem-based learning the course is content driven, students have little opportunity to define their own learning needs and much of the work is done by students working individually and interacting with the tutor. This then dissolves any notion of dialogic learning that is seen by many as vital to the problem-based approach.

A further model described by Mason is the *Wrap Around model* or the 50/50 model, since here, tailor-made materials are wrapped around existing materials, and online interactions and discussions occupy half the students' time. Thus what we see in practice are students engaging with online activities and discussions supported by existing textbooks, articles, resources and tutorials. The tutor's role is more demanding, because unlike the Content + Support model less of the course is predetermined, or provided in some kind of 'knowledge repository', and tutors are required to interact with the students through the online activities and discussions. There is a sense that this model offers students more of an online community and tutors can facilitate students on a one to one or small group basis and the course is created through these interactions. The danger here, however, is that what at first seems to be problem-based learning is actually problem-solving learning, and this confusion can cause disjunction for students between the expectation of autonomy and the control exerted by the tutor.

Finally, Mason suggested the *Integrated model* whereby online discussion, processing information and undertaking tasks are central to the course, with the consequence that course content, because the students largely determine it, is both fluid and dynamic. This kind of approach is more akin to liquid learning (Savin-Baden, 2007) which is characterized by emancipation, reflexivity and flexibility so that knowledge and knowledge boundaries are contestable and always on the move. Bauman (2000) has argued that we have moved into liquid modernity, an era characterized by the social and technological changes that occurred since the 1960s, embodied by the sense of living in constant change, ambivalence and uncertainty. In an integrated course knowledge and learning are thus seen as dynamic. Courses comprise learning resources, collaborative activities and joint assignments in ways that create a learning community by reducing the distinction between content and support, and promoting a course content defined by the student cohort. In practice, activities are carried out on the Web using resources supplied by tutors, external links and real-time events. The interactive nature of such courses means that students can integrate components of discussion conferences, along with personal reflections, into their assignments. This model would seem to be the one that fits most effectively with problem-based learning. However, a different way of considering this would be to locate problem-based learning for use in an online setting as a series of constellations (Table 6.1).

Constellations of PBLonline

The idea of locating different formulations of PBLonline on line as a series of constellations is because many of them relate to one another and overlap in particular configurations or patterns. Further, they also share characteristics in terms of some forms of focus on knowledge, more or less emphasis on the process of learning and the fact that each constellation begins by focusing on some kind of problem scenarios. The notion constellation helps us to see that there are patterns not just within the types of PBLonline but across the different constellations.

What is particularly important also, are the modes of knowledge in operation, as delineated in Table 6.2.

CONSTELLATION I: PROBLEM-SOLVING LEARNING

Problem-solving learning is more than just finding a solution to a given problem, indeed it is the type of teaching many staff have been using for years. The focus is upon giving students a lecture or an article to read and then a set of questions based upon the information given. Students are expected to find the solutions to these answers and bring them to a seminar as a focus for discussion. Problem scenarios here are set within and bounded

Table 6.1 Constellations of PBLonline

	Constellation 1 Problem-solving learning	Constellation 2 Problem-based learning for knowledge management	Constellation 3 Project-led problem-based learning	Constellation 4 Problem-based learning for practical capabilities	Constellation 5 Problem-based learning for critical understanding	Constellation 6 Problem-based learning for multimodal reasoning	Constellation 7 Collaborative distributed problem-based learning	Constellation 8 Cooperative distributed problem-based learning	Constellation 9 Problem-based learning for transformation and social reform
Problem type	Linear	Designed to promote cognitive competence	Project-led	Practical resolution	Knowledge with action	Managing dilemmas	Defined by team in relation to practice	Defined by team in relation to assignment	Seeing alternatives
Level of interaction	Problem-focused	Problem-focused	Project team	Practical action	Integrations of knowledge and skills across boundaries	Taking a critical stance	Collaborative	Cooperative	Exploring structures and beliefs
Focus of knowledge	Mode 1	Mode 1	Mode 2	Mode 2	Mode 1 and 2	Mode 3	Mode 4	Mode 4	Mode 4 and 5
Form of facilitation	Directive	Directive	Project management	Guide to practice	Coordinator of knowledge and skills	Orchestrator of learning opportunities	Enabler of group reflection	Consultant to team	Decoder of cultures
Focus of assessment	Solving of problem	Testing of knowledge	Project management	Competence for the world of work	Use of capabilities across contexts	Integrate capabilities across disciplines	Self analysis self-peer-tutor	Collaborative	Flexible and student-led
Learning emphasis	Achievement of task	Knowledge management	Completion of project	Development of capabilities	Synthesis across boundaries	Critical thought	Effective team work	High team support	Interrogation of frameworks

Table 6.2 Modes of knowledge

Mode 1	Propositional knowledge that is produced within academe separate from its use, with the academy being considered as the traditional environment for the generation of this form of knowledge.
Mode 2	Knowledge that transcends disciplines and is produced in, and validated through, the world of work.
Mode 3	Knowing in and with uncertainty, a sense of recognizing epistemological gaps that increase uncertainty
Mode 4	Disregarded knowledge, spaces in which uncertainty and gaps are recognized along with the realization of the relative importance of gaps between different knowledge and different knowledge hierarchies
Mode 5	Holding diverse knowledges with uncertainties

Source: From Savin-Baden, 2007.

by a discrete subject or disciplinary area. In some curricula students are given specific training in problem-solving techniques, but in many cases they are not. The focus in this kind of learning is largely upon acquiring the answers expected by the lecturer, answers that are rooted in the information supplied in some way to the students. Thus the solutions are always linked to a specific curricula content, which is seen as vital for students to cover in order for them to be competent and effective practitioners. The solutions are therefore bounded by the content and students are expected to explore little extra material other than that provided, in order to discover the solutions. In practice this means that the kinds of online problems that will be provided for students will be linear in nature, have clear boundaries and possess only one correct answer. In Constellation 1 the role of the facilitator is to guide the team towards the answer, direct them away from avenues that might distract them, and to help them towards discovering knowledge that will aid them to solve the problem the answer to which is already known by the facilitator.

CONSTELLATION 2: PROBLEM-BASED LEARNING FOR KNOWLEDGE MANAGEMENT

This constellation is characterized by a view of knowledge that is essentially propositional, with students being expected to become competent in applying knowledge in the context of solving, and possibly managing, problems. In this constellation students are not just expected to be able to solve the problem and find out the given answer; they are required to understand the knowledge. PBLonline is used as a means of helping students to learn the required curriculum content and enabling them to become competent in knowledge management. Knowledge is 'solid' and perceived by students as being 'out there' and largely independent of themselves as learners. Students will therefore see themselves as capable of receiving, reproducing and researching knowledge supplied by experts, and using PBLonline to develop their understanding of the relationship between that knowledge and its practical application.

CONSTELLATION 3: PROJECT-LED PROBLEM-BASED LEARNING

This constellation emerged from work undertaken with media practice educators in the UK. It is a model that becomes apparent from an exploration of the relationship between the use of 'live' project work in media practice and problem-based learning. The study began initially because of a realization of a conflict between the kinds of work-based learning that were being expected by external organizations that were skill-based, and the kinds of project-based learning occurring in universities. It proposes a model for work related learning that meets the needs of students, employers and educators. The study (Savin-Baden and Hanney, 2006) highlighted the need for a new model of problem-based learning that reflected the values of problem-based learning while also recognizing the value of 'Live Projects' or simulated work-related learning based on 'real world data'. In practice, this constellation focuses on students acquiring skills for practice in the context of a project that is work-related, such as producing a media artifact, which may involve a 'live' client brief. Thus it transcends Constellations 2 and 4 by utilizing project management tools to structure the problem-based learning exercise, where the technical knowledge and skills to be gained are clearly delineated by the tutor; but the learning is derived from utilizing opportunities, resources and experience in the workplace and is led by the participating students. Many of the skills here can be undertaken through online simulations and packages, but as with Constellation 4 it will need to be a blended approach.

CONSTELLATION 4: PROBLEM-BASED LEARNING FOR PRACTICAL
CAPABILITY

This constellation of problem-based learning has, as its overarching concept, the notion of practice. Students learn how to problem solve and to become competent in applying this ability to other kinds of problem scenarios and situations within given frameworks. Thus the students develop critical thinking skills for the workplace, interpreted somewhat narrowly as the ability to use problem-solving abilities in relation to propositional knowledge as a means of becoming competent in the workplace, and as being able to turn on these skills at any given point. The difficulty with this model of PBLonline is that it is not really possible to use it effectively at a distance. The nature of this form of PBLonline is its emphasis on practicality and thus practising skills must be part of it. Blended approaches can be used with such curricula, but it is important in these kinds of curricula to ensure that skills-based learning does not become a form of behavioural training in which competence to practise can be ticked off against a checklist. A further danger with this constellation is that PBLonline is being used to develop narrow sets of skills that may feel to the students as somewhat divorced from any other forms of knowledge. For example, an overemphasis on communication skills or teamwork, without students being encouraged to engage with and reflect upon the related theory and current research, can result in an uncritical acceptance of the guidance given by tutors. Critical games, web quests and critical discussion forums can help to overcome some of these difficulties.

CONSTELLATION 5: PROBLEM-BASED LEARNING FOR CRITICAL
UNDERSTANDING

In this constellation there is a shift away from a demand for mere know-how and propositional knowledge. Instead, problem-based learning becomes a vehicle to bridge the gap between models of thinking and actions, so that capabilities are developed in the form of being able to take a critical stance. In this constellation there is a shift away from a demand from knowledge management and practical action so that the student works, learns and develops *herself*. Learning is therefore seen here as knowing and under-standing knowledge from the disciplines, and also recognizing the relation-ship between them, so that a student can make sense for herself both personally and pedagogically. This kind of problem-based learning unites disciplines with skills (of all sorts), such that the student is able to see, from her stance as a future professional, the relationship between her personal stance and the propositional knowledge of the disciplines. She is enabled to develop not only an epistemological position but also a practice related perspective that integrates multiple ways of knowing and being.

These next constellations move the pedagogy and the curriculum towards a sense of uncontaining learning and reducing ordering in ways that fit better with PBLonline than more traditional models.

CONSTELLATION 6: PROBLEM-BASED LEARNING FOR MULTIMODAL
REASONING

Many authors (Bayne, 2005a, 2005b; Land and Bayne, 2005; Jewitt, 2005) have argued that the imagery seen on screen is having an increasing influence over the way in which we manage knowledge, and make sense and meaning in higher education. In this constellation problem-based learning is designed to enable students to transcend knowledge and capabilities in ways that are necessarily multimodal, so that through scenarios students recognize not only that text, disciplinary, screen, and bodily boundaries exist but that they are also somewhat illusory, that they have been erected. In this model tutors encourage students to develop their own stance towards these multimodal discourses and to reframe them for themselves, but without risking the reframing of the infrastructure of the disciplines. This model will work well with most forms of PBLonline where transdisciplinary learning is important, and particularly for modules situated in later years of degree programmes or early years of Master's studies.

CONSTELLATION 7: COLLABORATIVE DISTRIBUTED PROBLEM-BASED LEARNING

This constellation is based on the model by McConnell (2006: 48) whereby students work in learning teams in order to define a problem relating to some form of professional or personal practice issue. The focus in this constellation is therefore on working collaboratively on a problem that can be shared with other PBLonline teams. There is also a strong focus in understanding and critiquing the nature and complexity of teamwork, in order that team members are able to use this understanding to develop their own professional practice. Finally, students are expected to both self and peer assess and share their findings with one another. In this constellation there is a high emphasis on reflexivity and accountability to one another in terms of the development of one's own learning.

CONSTELLATION 8: COOPERATIVE DISTRIBUTED PROBLEM-BASED LEARNING

This constellation is also based on the model by McConnell (2006: 48); however, the focus here is on the development of learning through the course assignment in consultation with peers and tutors, and less on the definition of a problem defined by the PBLonline team as in constellation seven. The assignment itself is designed around a real issue the team face in professional practice as well as a component of the course being studied. There are many similarities here with constellation seven with a high emphasis being placed on team support and cooperation. However, there is a wider brief here in that the assignment contributes not only to the students' own professional practice but also to the course itself. Thus learning here is not only about the development of the students' personal and professional stance, but also that of the tutor and wider staff. This is a complex constellation but one that goes some way toward shifting the locus of power from staff toward the students.

CONSTELLATION 9: PROBLEM-BASED LEARNING FOR TRANSFORMATION AND SOCIAL REFORM

This form of PBLonline is one that seeks to provide for the students a kind of higher education that offers, within the curriculum, multiple models of action, knowledge, reasoning and reflection, along with opportunities for the students to challenge, evaluate and interrogate them. It embraces Pratt's notion of teaching for social reform (Pratt *et al.*, 1988) in which effective teaching is designed to change society in substantive ways. Through PBL-online here facilitators awaken students' embedded perspectives as well as the values and ideologies located in texts and common practices within their disciplines. Thus texts, in the broadest sense of the notion of 'texts' are interrogated for what is said and what is omitted; what is included and what is excluded, and students are encouraged to explore who and what is represented and omitted from dominant discourses.

This is a vital model for PBLonline because it shifts students away from more traditional models of online learning that focus on content coverage and ordering the learning in particular ways. In particular it encourages staff and students to explore the way in which the digital spaces that are created for staff (by commercial organizations that are politicized and contained by universities) and used by students enables, but perhaps more often occludes, ways of seeing where information is located. For as Bayne asks:

> If the spatial organization and visuality of the screen both represents and *creates* a value system and an ontology, what social and pedagogical practices does the VLE interface reflect, inform and inscribe? What meaning does it produce? What version of pedagogy does it 'make visible' and what alternatives does it blind us to?
>
> (Bayne, 2005b: 2)

Thus programmes, modules and scenarios are designed in this constellation in such a way as to prompt students to examine the underlying structures and belief systems implicit within a discipline or profession itself; in order not only to understand the disciplinary area but also its credence. The challenge here is to design learning that maximizes the use of VLEs, open source ware, games and 3D virtual worlds.

Step 4: Decide how you want students to learn

There are a number of different models of PBLonline, but the main difference is whether they are a blended or a distance model. Sharpe *et al.* (2006) delineate eight dimensions that seem to be present in blended learning, namely: delivery, technology, chronology, locus, roles, pedagogy, focus and direction. However, they suggest that there are three ways in which the terms are currently being used, summarized as follows:

1　The provision of supplementary resources for courses that are conducted on traditional lines through an institutionally supported virtual learning environment.

2   The use of technology to facilitate interaction and communication and replace other modes of teaching often underpinned by radical course designs.
3   '. . . students taking a holistic view of the interaction of technology and their learning, including the use of their own technologies, although this is currently under reported and under researched in higher education' (Sharpe *et al.*, 2006: 2–3).

Although there are blended courses where the focus on technology is high, and distance courses which include study weeks, in the main the difference between blended and distance is often a question of focus and philosophy. For example, one of the main difficulties with blended forms of PBLonline is managing the balance between face-to-face and online learning. Students in face-to-face programmes do not always see the value of discussion forums when much of their face-to-face learning is dialogic in nature, and they often feel discussion forums take up too much time. Thus, it is important with PBLonline in blended contexts that students do see the value in online learning. It is often best to use a blended PBLonline approach for sound reasons, such as:

1   Interprofessional learning with large cohorts divided across different sites and diverse disciplines.
2   Students undertaking sandwich years or fieldwork activities as part of their programme.
3   Large cohorts where students can work in small online teams and develop within them a community who share a common interest or passion.
4   Part-time programmes of study where online support and discussion helps to develop the community of learners who might otherwise only meet irregularly.

In terms of online at a distance, many of these programmes have a different ethos, since students have particular reasons for studying this way and appear to have a different commitment to online learning from those involved in blended programmes, although loneliness, technological barriers and being poorly trained and equipped do cause many distance students to struggle.

Step 5: Decide where you want students to learn using PBLonline

The decision to implement PBLonline largely tends to occur at modular level, late on in an undergraduate programme of study where it will be seen as low risk. Alternatively it may be undertaken as a module within a postgraduate or Masters' programme. There remain few fully PBLonline programmes, but the decision as to where to place PBLonline in terms of module, subject or programme depends too on the type of constellation adopted. Decisions about the location of PBLonline unfortunately all too often remain a case of achieving agreement at a faculty or institutional level on the basis of merely what will be seen as perilous and what will not.

Step 6: Decide types of scenarios

It would seem that different types of scenarios need to be used in online education from those used in problem-based face-to-face learning, ones that are pedagogically different, since online communication is more complex that face-to-face communication in small teams. Further, it might also be that online education results in a particular typology of problem-based learning that requires different scenarios. At one level the inter-linking of problem-based learning with virtual learning environments has brought creativity to problem-based learning and the development of innovative multimedia materials. However, it is clear from much of the literature that this is not always the case, and the focus on the achievement of outcomes and tasks is causing instead a narrowing of the definition of problem-based learning and a certain boundedness about the types of problem scenarios being adopted, and the way that problem-based learning is being used. The variety of PBLonline scenarios may be seen in terms of the following types, examples of which are provided in the Resources section:

1 Variety 1: Cases which tell a story about a patient.
2 Variety 2: Cases which provide a company/business related problem.
3 Variety 3: A number of different types of problems related to one particular topic area, for example a road traffic accident scene or a court scene.
4 Variety 4: Online games, for example those that can be played in a multi-user virtual environment such as Second Life.
5 Variety 5: Virtual patients: simulations or representations of individuals who are designed by facilitators as a means of creating a character in a health care setting. (These are discussed in depth in Chapter 7.)
6 Variety 6: Storyboards, adapted from the film industry to business, and used for planning and more recently in the fields of web and software development.
7 Variety 7: Interaction or Conversation Analysis. This is a written conversation that facilitates students in generating ideas, exploring subtext and interpreting text.
8 Variety 8: Podcasts have become popular as students and teachers can share information and students can see or listen to lectures again. Since podcasts are not real-time, students can revisit the material.
9 Variety 9: Picture collages are a series of overlaid images on a webpage that challenge students to consider their views on a particular issue, such as what counts as being a leader, teacher or astronomer.

It is important, however that scenarios are developed that shift students away from solid knowledge towards liquid learning.

Step 7: Decide the form of e-facilitation

Facilitation of the group at the start of the module is vital, so that students feel supported, but moderation can be seen by students who are familiar with problem-based learning as an interruption and not a support (as will be discussed in Chapter 5). Regular chat sessions are important to maintain interest and motivation for the problem-based learning teams, since synchronous teamwork supports the group process in problem-based learning much more effectively than the asynchronous discussion. This is because problem-based learning relies on the swift generation of ideas and responses and the continual commitment of the group to supporting one another in developing materials and guiding each other through the process of managing the problems.

Step 8: Decide on type and size of problem-based learning team

The size and type of the team does depend on how PBLonline is being used. For example, in Constellations 5–9 small groups work best: four to six students can work effectively to manage or solve a problem. However, for Constellations 1–4 where the focus on dialogic learning is usually lower than in other constellations, then up to ten students will work fairly successfully.

Step 9: Decide on the type and amount of resources

If courses are online and at a distance a series of readings is vital to support learning, yet in PBLonline it is important that students are encouraged to find, use and share resources. Thus, content focused online lectures and podcasts should be kept to a minimum so that students are enabled to take responsibility for their own learning and develop independence in inquiry. A comprehensive reading list with choice and minimal direction is probably one of the best resources for PBLonline.

Step 10: Plan implementation strategies

Implementation planning is the step that is most often omitted. Time and space in academic life is often excessively busy and the preparation for courses and sound implementation is restricted. A suggested schedule for implementation is outlined in Table 6.3. It allows for the practising of problem-based learning, with some initial educational development in the first 2 years for facilitators, which will then support them through the first year of implementation. In year three the whole curriculum is changed to PBL-online and ongoing support by an external consultant allows for readjustments to be made and facilitators to be supported through the change process. The inclusion of student preparation at the beginning of the first year when PBLonline is to be used is vital, so that the students understand the process. Ongoing commitment to student preparation and support is also essential so that they are helped to adjust to problem-based learning. The incorporation of an ongoing evaluation means that the findings of the evaluation can be used to make changes in the curriculum as it progresses. A model that works successfully for face-to-face problem-based learning (Savin-Baden, 2003) can be used for PBLonline in the way shown in Table 6.3.

Table 6.3 Implementation strategy

Year 1
- Three-day educational development workshops provided for all staff
- Optional extra workshop days provided with external consultant for development of scenarios and redesign of assessments to fit with learning approach
- Scenarios and resources designed for introduction into two modules

---

Year 2
- Problem-based learning introduced into one or two modules
- Students' ongoing evaluation of problem-based learning modules introduced: results to inform new curriculum
- Process of curriculum redesign commenced with focus on the content that staff want students to learn
- Learning intentions translated into curriculum levels with appropriate problem-based assessment
- Learning opportunities designed: problem-based learning sessions, games and webquests
- Meetings convened with professional body/colleagues to discuss planned changes

---

Year 3
- Two-week problem-based learning induction programme provided for first students
- Three-day educational development workshops provided for staff who missed first workshops or have recently joined university
- Monthly facilitator support group held with external consultant

---

Year 4
- Ongoing student preparation and support
- Curriculum revalidated
- Facilitator master classes commenced

Year 5
- Ongoing student preparation and support
- Scenarios and resources evaluated, new scenarios and materials developed
- Three-day educational development workshops provided for staff who have recently joined the university

---

Conclusion

However, effective PBLonline programmes for the future will need to consider transcending the modular system of higher education. Such programmes would enable students to engage with learning in a more integrated fashion than the current over-assessed, modular system. Learning through units with weekly team activities along with assessment that focuses on students' interests is more likely to result in transformation and social reform than the current over managed outcome-led system.

What it means to facilitate in a virtual context will depend upon a whole cluster of factors that include the type of online learning adopted, the values engendered in facilitation and the extent to which students are encouraged to develop student–student interaction through such programmes. It is to this subject that we turn in Chapter 7.

PBLonline futures

Introduction

This chapter seeks to present a challenge to the problem-based learning community about the possibilities for reinventing problem-based learning as both a philosophy and an approach to learning. What I offer is not just a constellation of questions and a number of big ideas, but instead some suggestions and priorities. It will be argued here that the notions of liminality and liquidity in the context of reconceptualization of learning spaces may offer some purchase on the questions and issues we face as a community and increasingly as an online learning community. This chapter will therefore suggest some options and possibilities, but it will begin by arguing that we need to see the shifts required as being located in the realms of 'new collegiality' and akin to a Second Life for problem-based learning. This is not only because it is a transformational position but also because we need to engage more deeply with Web 2.0 technologies and learning in liminal spaces such as 3D worlds. However, it will be argued that:

1   We need to reinvent PBLonline as a much more troublesome learning space than it is already.
2   Learning spaces are increasingly absent in problem-based learning online.

New collegiality and new learning spaces?

Recent literature on change has documented a diversity of approaches but they are largely seen in polarized terms within higher education as either top down or bottom up approaches. Berg and Östergren (1979) have argued that bottom up components, in this case the staff, should lead the innovation and managers should play a facilitating role. However, in the context of implementing PBLonline it is perhaps better to utilize what Elton (1996) refers to as new collegiality. In new collegiality the innovation would be managed as both a top-down and bottom-up approach and this innovation reflects Elton's suggestions in the following ways:

- *Information should be freely available to all*: Information about key decisions both top-down and bottom-up must be available to all involved, including library staff who are vital in terms of the resources for problem-based learning.
- *Decision making should be undertaken by the team*: the decisions about curriculum design and the particular constellation model of problem-based learning to be adopted should be made by both staff and management together.
- *Academic staff will be knowledgeable about the change*: all staff must be supplied with information and suggestions about the possibilities for implementation and collaborative decision making.
- *There will be trust in the professionalism of those involved*: problem scenarios and modules should be designed by various groups of staff who are trusted to follow the guidelines and suggestions already made in the corporate decision making processes.
- *Academic tasks will be viewed equally*: although most staff are generally involved in the design process, this is one area of collegiality that often does not work. There is invariably disagreement across the faculty about the relative value of teaching, curriculum design and research. Elton does point out that this will be difficult to achieve 'in view of the strongly entrenched disciplinary loyalties and associated research attitudes, but are all the more important for that' (Elton, 1996: 141).

The adoption of many of the principles of new collegiality will mean that what occurs in practice is a form of distributed decision-making across the boundaries of the university and discipline-based hierarchies. The future possibilities for using PBLonline, particularly in the context of social software characterized through the Web 2.0 and Web 3.0 movements is immense, and tends to transcend hierarchical boundaries as staff and students together become knowledge, or content, producers. The impact of wikis, blogs and learning in 3D virtual worlds on the PBL community remains relatively under explored, and the following section suggests ideas and exemplars about how PBL might be used differently in the future. Thus, problem-based learning needs to be reinvented as a more troublesome learning space because of the challenges of these new and emerging technologies and the influence they are having on staff, students and what 'learning' means. However, it is suggested that in moving towards adopting PBLonline that engages students and staff in learning which reflects social networking, we need to acknowledge the loss of learning spaces and recognize the importance of liminality in learning.

The concept of learning spaces (Savin-Baden, 2007) expresses the idea that there are diverse forms of spaces within the life and life world of the academic, where opportunities to reflect and analyse their own learning position occur. Such learning spaces are places of engagement where often disconnected thoughts and ideas that have been inchoate, begin to cohere as a result of the creation of some kind of suspension from daily life. In such spaces, staff and students often recognize that their perceptions of learning, teaching, knowledge and identity are being challenged and realize that they have to make a decision about their response to such challenges. Yet such often hidden spaces are invariably not valued by university leadership nor recognized as being important in our media populated culture. Learning spaces are often places of transition, and sometimes transformation, where the individual experiences some kind of shift or reorientation in their life world. While these kinds of shifts are apparent in some problem-based learning curricula, if PBL is to survive in this late modern world we need to embrace troublesome knowledge and engage with liminality. The state of liminality tends to be characterized by a stripping away of old identities, an oscillation between states and personal transformation. Liminal spaces are thus suspended states and serve a transformative function, as someone moves from one state or position to another. It could be argued that learning in 3D worlds has a liminal quality about it because of learning with and through an avatar, yet in the context of PBLonline such liminality in learning is rarely noticed or valued. The importance of acknowledging learning spaces and engaging with liminality in learning is that it will enable us as facilitators to reconsider, value and utilize those challenges of different forms of embodiment, students becoming stuck and learning in different ways in the context of new constellations of problem-based learning.

Beyond the VLE?

Digital spaces have also resulted in discussions and concerns about both containment and exteriorization in online environments. Containment is particularly evident in virtual learning environments (VLEs) such as WebCT and Blackboard that structure and manage learning. While many learning technologists have argued that academics experience difficulty because they do not know how to use VLEs in innovative ways, academics see their difficulty as believing the technology disables rather than enables the pedagogy. Thus, creativity is prevented through the quest for linearity and maintenance of control. As Lyotard remarked, 'knowledge and power are simply two sides of the same questions: who decides what is knowledge, and who knows what needs to be decided? In the computer age, the question of knowledge is now more than ever a question of government' (Lyotard, 1979).

Virtual learning environments do not easily allow for liquidity in terms of changing structures and visuality – and although this is increasingly possible in some VLEs, it is relatively rarely undertaken by lecturers and for many the semiotic impact is something they are not attuned to. Further, to change the structure and the appearance, to remove what is 'normal,' is usually disliked by both the VLE designers and the university management hierarchy – for to allow emancipation is to allow too much risk in a world where increasingly 'corporateness' is all. Yet as Kress (2007) recently remarked:

- the relationship between writing and image has changed;
- relationship between author and authority has/is fraying;
- we no longer have pages but only metaphors, for example, websites;
- we are no longer readers but visitors;
- a footnote might be the same as a hyperlink.

As Kress has suggested, not only are technology and culture always closely linked, but also cultural resources are involved in the shaping of technologies in the first place; at the same time that cultural resources locate the application and transformation of that technology. Thus, as he suggests:

> If we regard learning as a process where 'what is (to be) learned' and 'what is available for the learner's engagement' is shaped by the environments in which learning takes place, we might be able to get closer to disentangling technological effects and cultural and social environments of various kinds, from those things which maybe remain relatively constant – for instance, the human processes of learning.
>
> (Kress, 2007)

Since the emergence of the Web 2.0 movement in 2004 there has been considerable debate about what constitutes Web 2.0 and what does not. Yet it would seem that the growth of this movement is liquid in nature and is something that is constantly developing and emerging differently. O'Reilly (2005) has argued that it 'doesn't have a hard boundary, but rather a gravitational core'. Others suggest that it does not refer to one development, but rather a series of emergent technologies such as Google, flickr, del.icio.us, wikis and blogs. However, as Alexander argues, 'Ultimately, the label "Web 2.0" is far less important than the concepts, projects and practices included in its scope' (Alexander, 2006: 33). Nevertheless, it would seem that we may be moving very quickly into Web 3.0 technologies, whereby the focus is on content. 'Generation C' is being used to capture the idea that we live in an age of content producers. There is also a further shift to include not just content but context. For example, Cook (2007) has argued for the notion of Generation CX to capture this and Bruns (2007) has suggested that we are in the realms of 'produsage'; a core activity of Generation C (and also possibly CX) and characterized by:

- Community-Based – produsage proceeds from the assumption that the community as a whole, if sufficiently large and varied, can contribute more than a closed team of producers, however qualified they may be.
- Fluid Roles – producers participate as is appropriate to their personal skills, interests, and knowledges; this changes as the produsage project proceeds.
- Unfinished Artefacts – content artefacts in produsage projects are continually under development, and therefore always unfinished; their development follows evolutionary, iterative, palimpsestic paths.
- Common Property, Individual Merit – contributors permit (non-commercial) community use, adaptation, and further development of their intellectual property, and are rewarded by the status capital they gain through this process.

(Bruns, 2007: 4)

Pedagogically these developments have created new kinds of digital spaces, and such pedagogical formulations as wikis and particularly del.icio.us enable staff and students to not only set up their own social and academic bookmarking but also to share bookmarks, find academics with similar interests and create new research collaborations.

PBL in 3D virtual worlds

To date problem-based learning has been seen as a relatively stable approach to learning, delineated by particular characteristics. Second Life PBL (SL/PBL) embraces not only Web 2.0 technologies but also troublesomeness and new curriculum learning spaces. The reason we need to reinvent problem-based learning as a more troublesome learning space is because of the challenges of new and emerging technologies and the impact they are having on staff, students and what 'learning' means. Whether it is through podcasts, wikis or mobile learning, learning is on the move. Further, it could be argued, and increasingly is, that cyberspace has resulted in a sense of multiple identities and disembodiment, or even different forms of embodiment. The *sense* of anonymity and the assumption that this was what was understood through one's words rather than one's bodily presence, is becoming increasingly unmasked through worlds such as Second Life. Yet in the process of trying out new identities in virtual 3D worlds, what I would term our representative identities, questions arise about the impact of these representative identities on our physical, embodied or place-based identities. What is also important in the whole issue of 3D worlds such as Second Life is: (a) the pedagogy of such worlds; and (b) the pedagogical possibilities underlying these worlds.

For example, it might be that 3D worlds and gaming not only have different, or diverse, underlying pedagogies (and pedagogical possibilities), but also assumptions are made about issues of power and control in games where avatars are representative of 'someone else', as opposed to a representation of one's own identities.

Scenarios and games

Games are usually described as exercises in which individuals co-operate or compete within a given set of rules (Jacques, 2000), such as charades, tiddlywinks or hockey, thus players act as themselves. A simulation is when a scenario is provided that in some way represents real life. The confusions that occur between problem-based learning and simulations relate to the use of real-life situations. In problem-based learning students are (usually) provided with real-life scenarios, they are expected to act as themselves and the situations with which they are presented are tailored according to the level of the course. In simulations individuals are ascribed roles related to the simulations, such as 'you are the manager of an engineering firm', or 'your aim in this simulation is to win the most money', with the tutor acting as a referee. Previously I have suggested that the use of games in problem-based learning is often inappropriate, as this changes the nature of problem-based learning and the focus of it as an approach to learning (Savin-Baden, 2000, 2003). For example, the original aims of this approach, as mentioned in the introduction, were to focus on complex, real world situations that have no one 'right' answer as the organizing focus for learning. Yet in the context of Web 2.0 learning, games and simulations can increase students' motivation for learning and facilitate team building. In particular, they are vital for team building in the initial stages of problem-based learning in virtual worlds. An example of a problem-based learning game used in Second Life is presented below.

SL PBL game

To date problem-based learning has been seen as a relatively stable approach to learning, delineated by particular characteristics. Most of the explanations of and arguments for problem-based learning, to date, have tended to focus on (or privilege) the cognitive perspectives over the ontological positions of the learner. This game is located in a new formulation of problem-based learning, namely Second Life PBL (SL/PBL), which embraces not only Web 2.0 technologies but also troublesomeness and new curriculum learning spaces.

This game is part of a PBL module in SL, which comprises four problem scenarios, as demonstrated in Table 7.1. The game is located in the single

Table 7.1 Overview of the SL/PBL module

Week	Activity	Location
Week 1	Warm-up PBL problem in allotted groups	Discussion board
Week 2	Scenario 1	Discussion in allocated groups MSN chat × 1
Week 3	Scenario 1 (continued) Second Life orientation activity	MSN chat × 2
Week 4	Scenario 2	Discussion
Week 5	Scenario 2 (continued)	Chat sessions × 3
Week 6	Scenario 2 (continued) Second Life treasure hunt	Second Life
Week 7	Scenario 3 Second Life game	Second Life
Week 8	Scenario 3 (continued)	Second Life
Week 9	Scenario 3 (continued)	Second Life
Week 10	Scenario 4 Designing your wiki	Discussion board, writeboards, chat
Week 11	Presentation of group wiki	Discussion board or Second Life
Week 12	Synthesis of group interaction	Writeboards

module approach to problem-based learning (Savin-Baden and Major, 2004) and Constellation 9, Problem-based learning for transformation and social reform (see Chapter 6). The type of problem scenarios used are those based on the adapted taxonomy in Table 7.2 below. Schmidt and Moust (2000) suggested a taxonomy for using problems in order to acquire different kinds of knowledge, rather than solving problems or covering subject matter. The importance of the work undertaken by Schmidt and Moust (2000) is not only the way they provide and explicate different problem types, but also their exploration of the way in which the questions asked of students guide the types of knowledge in which students engage. This module begins with a focus on explanatory problems, but later focuses on personal knowledge with particular reference to dilemmas located within the game.

In practice, students will work in teams of five over a 3-week module and will be facilitated by a tutor using the pragmatic enabler approach (Wilkie, 2002), which emphasizes learning processes rather than content acquisition. The aim of this approach to facilitation is to enable students to achieve their maximum potential, thus the forms of facilitation are time and context dependent and responsive to the needs of students.

Table 7.2 Types of knowledge and types of problems

Explanatory knowledge	Descriptive knowledge	Procedural knowledge	Personal knowledge
Types of problems			
Explanation problem	Fact-finding problem	Strategy problem	Moral dilemma problem
Examples			
People in the fifteenth century used to believe it was possible to fall off the edge of the known world	Following recent political changes relating to land use in Zimbabwe many internal borders have changed	A 43-year-old woman cannot lift her right arm more than 45 degrees and she complains of pins and needles in her hand	A mother breaks into a chemist's shop at night to obtain life-saving drugs for her baby. She contacts her local physician the next day to explain what she has done
Example of question			
Explain why	What would a legal map look like?	If you were this client's physiotherapist what would you do?	What should the doctor do?

Source: Adapted from Schmidt and Moust, 2000: 68.

Explanation of playing the game

1   The game has 48 cards, each in the form of a biographical notecard about a different person, their work and home life, and their medical condition, arranged in four types (suits) of 12.
2   Students work in teams of 5.
3   The cards are located on a large video type screen on SL and when touched turn around (each student team will have their own board but all the characters/cards will be the same on each board).
4   The idea is to touch the cards but only four cards (the first one touched from each suit) will turn over, revealing a 'family':

   • Diamonds – First generation (Grandparents)
   • Hearts – Second generation (Parents)
   • Spades – Third generation (Children)
   • Clubs – Additional member from any generation.

5   The students then touch the joker at the bottom of the screen, who will identify one of the suits. This is the family member and the medical condition they then have to manage in the role of a health and social care professional.

The students

This game is designed for final year undergraduate students or Master's students.

Learning principles of this game

1   Learning the skill of learning to learn in SL is a component of the game.
2   Making collaborative decisions as a team is an important goal.
3   The characters in the game are people with whom the students can identify.
4   Uncertainty and exploration are part of the game.
5   Dialogue is central to the game since dialogue facilitation games improve students' conceptual understanding through dialogue rather than through competition.
6   Ludus and paidea in the SL/PBL game are combined so the players can move between the two. Frasca sees paidea as 'a physical or mental activity which has no immediate useful objective, nor defined objective, and whose only reason to be is based in the pleasure experienced by the player.' Whereas ludus is seen as an 'activity organized under a system of rules that defines a victory or a defeat, a gain or a loss' (Frasca, 1999, cited in Newman, 2004:19–20).
7   Engagement with disjunction and foreign knowledge are central components of the game. Perkins suggests foreign knowledge is due to:

> Difficulty with understanding new content often arises because current belief systems are comfortably familiar and sometimes deeply entrenched, making the new content appear bizarre or alien. An example mentioned earlier is the problem of presentism in teaching history. Students tend to view past events through the lens of contemporary understandings, not easily putting on the mindsets of times and cultures past.
>
> (Perkins, in press)

Learning intentions of the game: the theory

1   To enable students to engage in collaborative learning in the context of SL/PBL.
2   To help students learn from one another about the roles and cultures of different professionals in health and social care.
3   To encourage discussing the notion of what counts as family.
4   To prompt students to explore personal perspectives about the concept of family.
5   To facilitate students in discussions about the impact of one family member's illness on other family members.

6   To help students to develop and present a means of managing the prob-
    lem scenario.
7   To provide an opportunity for students to develop a family-centred
    intervention programme.

Playing the game

This game has been designed not only to help you to learn collaboratively
but also to understand each other's professional perspectives and roles.
Through the course of the game it is expected that you will work as an
effective team and that you will develop a considered position about what
counts as a family in today's society. In order to play the game you will first
need to follow the pre-game instructions:

Pre-game instructions for students

1   Download Second Life.
2   Dress your avatar.
3   Find Coventry University Island: http://slurl.com/secondlife/Coventry
    %20University/144/119/51.
4   Explore Coventry University Island and find:

    a   the beach;
    b   the game.

5   Meet in your team in Second Life at a time decided mutually between
    the team for not more than 2 hours.

Game instructions

This game is designed to help you to learn to work as a team, to make
collaborative decisions, to discuss the concept of family and to design an
appropriate option for the family you are working with. Therefore your task,
should you choose to accept it, is:

1   Meet as a team of five to six students (you will be allocated to a team but
    you may negotiate its makeup before you begin the task).
2   Explore the game.
3   Meet for 2 hours a week as a team using a mode of your choice.
4   Discuss the issues raised by the people on the game board.
5   Create a list of group learning needs.
6   Research and share your learning needs.
7   Work as a team to produce an intervention for this family that you can
    present in a group wiki in 3 weeks time for a team assessment.
8   You will also be expected to present a transcript of your Second Life and
    any discussions or chat sessions to enable your team to be assessed.

Figure 7.1
The location of
the game on the
Coventry University
Island

Figure 7.2
The learning space for
students to work in
groups, this is one of
several spaces

Figure 7.3
A close-up of the
game

This game presents a possibility of adapting problem-based learning in a way that engages with Web 2.0 technologies and learning in 3D worlds. It illustrates a means of creating new curriculum spaces that help students to embrace contemporary dislocations and mediate rhetoric differently.

Other applications that support the use of PBL in Web 2.0 spaces

There are many other sources that can support ways of using PBLonline in diverse and innovative ways; this section delineates just a few of the more recent developments.

Infiniteams

This is a system that operates in real-time, with users working together either remotely or in the same office. Teams of three to eight people can participate at the same time, using one PC per person. Although the main focus of its use to date has been on leadership development and team building, it can be adapted for use with PBLonline. The team is located on a remote island and then provided with a number of challenges with which the team must engage. The authors TPLD (Team Play Learning Dynamics) argue that this game:

- allows teams to collaborate remotely;
- can be used across a wide range of courses;
- allows teams to learn skills required for effective remote teaming.

This learning environment is built around team development principles and the software automatically records conversations and actions that can be effectively used, along with the facilitator's real time observations, to assess both team and individual capabilities in critical areas such as problem-solving and decision-making.

Labyrinth and virtual patients

This is an experimental educational narrative pathway authoring system being developed at the University of Edinburgh along with a number of other partners. Users are presented with a set of randomly selected choices as they move through a Labyrinth, each of which has a consequence for the user. Examples include virtual patients, quizzes, games and tutorials. Labyrinth is an online activity modelling system that allows users to build interactive 'game informed' educational activities such as virtual patients, simulations, games, mazes and algorithms. It has been designed to be adaptable and simple to use while retaining a wealth of game-like features. An example of the use of Labyrinth is provided by Ellaway et al. (2004), who explain the development of virtual patients in three distinct forms and respective applications:

1   Virtual patients for research: these are computer simulations that explore the effect of drugs in humans.
2   Electronic Patient Records (EPRs) which comprise the storage of data relating to patients.
3   Virtual patients for education: used for problem-based learning, so that these virtual patients normally include both the patient and their context.

Conclusion

At the end of this text I suggest we need to try to work out for ourselves how we want to be in these spaces and how we want to communicate with others who are there already. Inevitably, we have sometimes got stuck, so what are the futures?

Possible futures

We can ignore all this and pretend it isn't happening.
We can lurk on the edges.
We can change everything immediately.

Preferred futures

We could consider our discipline-based pedagogies or our curricula (why we teach physics the way we teach it, for example) and consider how we might reinvent problem-based learning in ways that embrace social networking and new spaces. We need to be aware that to ignore the ways that students are choosing to learn and interact through social networking outside the class room will result in losing them in the classroom.

This chapter suggests that perhaps problem-based learning communities can embrace some of these ideas and concepts in order to enhance their distinctiveness. Most of the explanations of and arguments for problem-based learning, to date, have tended to focus on (or privilege) the cognitive perspectives over the ontological positions of the learner. Perhaps the future of problem-based learning lies in no longer lurking with solid knowledge and cognitive stances and but instead in focusing on the contestable nature of knowledge.

Part 3

Resources

Building online teams

Building teams in face-to-face problem-based settings is an area which has gained increasing attention in the problem-based learning community. However, it has been recognized that building online teams requires considerably more effort than face-to-face teams, in order to ensure that the problem-based teams work effectively together (for example, Savin-Baden and Wilkie, 2006). Advocates of collaborative, co-operative or team learning argue that there are several essential components for effective learning teams (Johnson *et al.*, 1998):

- Positive interdependence, meaning that team members need each other to succeed. All members of the team must be involved and committed to team success, although it could be argued that a larger team could still be successful even if there were a passenger or two in the team.
- Promote interactions, implying that interaction between and among team members should be designed to promote the members and the team. Team members help each other, provide feedback for ongoing improvement and encourage an atmosphere of openness to diversity and new ideas.
- Individual accountability, indicating that even though functioning and normally being assessed on team processing and performance, individual students must be held accountable for their work and on their individual contributions to the team.
- Undertaking reflection, as a team at the conclusion of a problem in order to identify their strengths and weaknesses and ensuring improvement next time.

The reason that the word 'team' is used rather than 'group' is because a team is a group of people organized to meet together, and:

1 The team has a *purpose* or purposes:

  - to disburse information;
  - to have a discussion – an open exchange of views;

- to make decisions – you are not a team unless you make some decisions together.

2   A team has a *limited membership* – if you change one person, you change the team.
3   A team has a *context* – a time and a geography.

Much of what occurs in PBLonline tends to resemble the following types of teams:

1   the tutor guided learning team;
2   the reflexive team;
3   the co-operative team;
4   the collaborative learning team.

The tutor guided learning team

This type of team is very much guided by the facilitator who sees their role as being to guide the students through each component of the problem. Thus students see problem scenarios as being set within or bounded by a discrete subject or disciplinary area. In some situations the tutor actually provides hints and tips on problem-solving techniques, the argument being that students very often have few skills to help them solve the problems they will encounter. The result is that solutions are often seen by students as being linked to specific curricula content.

The reflexive team

This kind of learning team is largely based on co-operative models of problem-based learning and Freireian forms of pedagogy (Freire, 1972, 1974; hooks, 1994). For example, in this type of team, working together is often talked about in terms of a journey but it is seen as less stable, less convergent and less collaborative than the existing literature relating to groups and group theory would imply. Reflexivity here is seen as an organizing principle, and thus it involves explicit shared reflection about the team process and findings of the learning needs of the team, rather than the masking of the kinds of paradox and conflict that emerge at almost every stage of most learning teams. Students in such teams are expected to feel able to point to unease connected both with their role within the team, the relationship between their individual concerns (that may stand in direct conflict with the collective ethos of the team), and the nature of support within the team. In these types of teams, therefore, each member is valued, and the optimum setting is created for ideas to grow, and individuals are empowered through affirmation. Thus the team serves as an interactive function for the individual. Through the team the individual is enabled to learn both through the experience of others and the appreciation of other people's life-worlds; and by reflecting upon these, to relate them to their own. Thus individual students, by making themselves and their learning the focus of reflection and analysis within the team, are able to value alternative ways of knowing. Dialogue here is central to progress in people's lives and it is through dialogue that values are deconstructed and reconstructed, and experiences relived and explored, in order to make sense of roles and relationships.

The co-operative team

In an extensive meta-analysis that included hundreds of studies, Johnson *et al.* (1991) concluded that collaborative learning arrangements were superior to competitive, individualistic structures on a variety of outcomes such as higher academic achievement, higher-level reasoning, more frequent generation of new ideas and solutions, and greater transfer of learning from one situation to another. The difference between co-operative learning and collaborative learning is that co-operative learning involves small group work to maximize student learning. This approach tends to maintain traditional lines of knowledge and authority whereas collaborative learning is based on notions of social constructivism.

The collaborative learning team

This is probably the most common form of learning seen in problem-based tutorials. Although it could be viewed as largely based on models of collaborative inquiry, there is still an element of tutor's control here. For example, the focus is on the development of specific levels of skills and thus small-team social skills are essential for successful collaboration in the problem-based learning environment. In addition to being able to communicate clearly with, accept and support all other team members individually, and resolve conflicts, students must be able to elicit each other's viewpoints and perspectives, question each other's assumptions and evidence, make decisions, manage the 'business' of the team and often make presentations to the larger year group.

Activities that help to build teams online include:

1   warm-up activities, such as introducing oneself, sharing something unusual about oneself or situation;
2   playing online team games;
3   doing competitive inter-team quizzes online;
4   designing team building activities for other teams in the cohort;
5   sharing interesting websites;
6   creating an innovative space, such as through writeboards;

7   giving each team member a different online activity or game which they need to critique and then share with the rest of the team.

What is important about activities that build teams is that the facilitator should let the team work on the activities themselves and not interrupt the process. Interruptions and distractions can quickly destroy the team building.

Scenarios that work

This section will consider the nature of problem scenarios in problem-based learning online. The issue of what might count as a problem and the complexity of problem design is something that is a challenge to many tutors implementing problem-based learning, whether face-to-face or in online contexts. Some people design the problems themselves; others use templates or download problems that can be adapted. This section will illustrate a number of scenarios that work well online and will demonstrate the way in which links and supporting material are used to enhance team collaboration.

Tips on writing scenarios for PBLonline

1   Keep them simple.
2   Provide a context for the scenario that will help students to understand the problem.
3   Link them with the learning intentions/objectives of the module.
4   Ensure they have current relevance to your subject.
5   Make them interesting enough to be a challenge but not so controversial that students become side-tracked.
6   Ensure they transcend discipline boundaries.
7   Consider how the scenario relates to other areas of the curriculum that are occurring simultaneously.
8   Locate and upload the kinds of resources students will require – but not too much, it is important to avoid the creation of a knowledge repository.
9   Ensure that scenarios vary across the levels of the course in both type and medium.

Types of scenarios/problems for PBLonline

Variety 1: Cases which tell a story about a patient

For example, the psychology department at the Erasmus University, Rotterdam (EUR) developed PsyWeb, a Learning Content Management

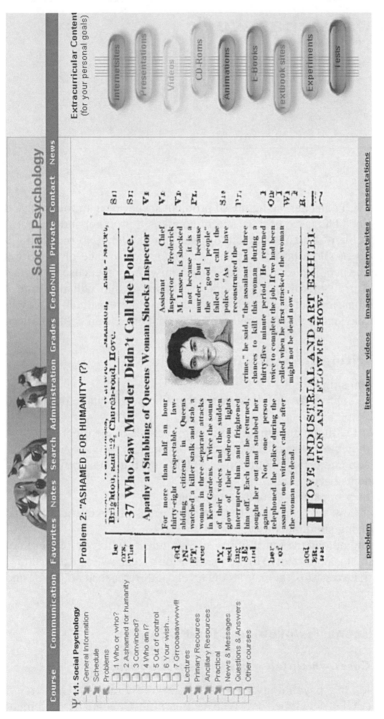

Figure R.1 A psychology problem, but the webpage illustrates the way in which students are supported in managing their resources through the tools available. From Savin-Baden, M. and Wilkie, K., *Problem-based Learning Online*, 2006. Reproduced with permission of Open University Press.

System that manages all curricular content. PsyWeb builds on research findings in educational psychology, cognitive psychology, and instructional design, and is specifically aimed at supporting student learning activities during self-study. Problem-based learning, as implemented at the EUR, is primarily used as a collaborative form of learning aimed at acquiring and organizing subject-matter. The scenario in Figure R.1, provided by te Winkel *et al.* (2006) is a psychology problem, and the webpage illustrates the way in which students are supported in managing their resources through the tools available in the system designed specifically to support PBLonline.

Variety 2: Cases which provide a company-/business-related problem

Example 1: PBLonline Scenario in Nursery Management (designed and supplied by Petra Luck, Liverpool Hope University)

One of the Parents/Carers in Family A works for an international firm and has received an offer of employment in Europe. She is given the choice of relocation for herself and her family in Italy, France or Finland. She has contacted 'Childcare Solutions' and requested that you, in your role as consultants, advise her about the types of childcare and education provision available in these countries. Your advice will include a recommendation as to which country could best meet the needs of her family. You should prepare a group response in the form of a formal report of approximately 2,000 words that reflects all individual group members' contributions. The group response should be completed by the 22 October 2006 and submitted via Learnwise.

Key concepts

- Family policies.
- Childcare entitlements.
- Parental contribution to fees.
- Range of provision.
- Main differences in education and care.
- Starting age.
- Integrated education and care systems.
- Philosophies of childhood.
- Children's rights and entitlements.

Example 2: PBLonline Scenario in Computing (provided by Beaumont and Chew, 2006)

This problem-based learning scenario (see Box R.1) consists of a computer network security scenario, involving both theory and practical work. Students

---

Box R.1 Problem statement

Your company's core business is offshore petroleum drilling, where the floating rigs are located in the North Sea off Scotland, UK. The company has recently designed and tested a new method of drilling that would increase drilling output by 250 per cent; this was documented and stored electronically. The drilling process is still undergoing refinement and its results are documented online with servers located in London, UK. Rival Oil companies are aware of the new innovations from your company and it is rumoured that they will by all means try to obtain any information regarding the technologies used.

Your department, Information Systems Security, is tasked to review the current security concerns of each department and the data centre (London).

The London HQ has various departments supporting the company functions; all the users have access to the Internet from their local ISP. The company has other supporting business partners that supply regular chemicals for its processing site, these companies transact online with your company web application services.

Your team is to provide recommendation(s) to improve on various security issues on the WAN, bearing in mind the rival companies have huge resources to conduct electronic espionage or disrupt your company's operations. You are also required to demonstrate a mock-up of WAN security for presentation to the senior management and document the risks and controls you recommend to deal with them. Your CEO will be present in this presentation and he is interested in how it is going to be managed.

---

are required to identify risks and threats for the scenario and design a secure infrastructure. Both the UK and Singapore sides of each team also had to construct logically identical demonstration networks using five PCs and associated network software/hardware.

Other sources of information

David, T. (1993). *Educational Provision for Our Youngest Children: European Perspectives*. Paul Chapman.

Gura, P. (1997). *Reflections on Early Education and Care*, inspired by Reggio Emelia. BAECE.

Oberheumer, P. and Ulich, M. (1997). *Working with Young Children in Europe*. Paul Chapman.

Penn, H. (1997). *Comparing Nurseries: Staff and Children in Italy, Spain and the UK*. Paul Chapman.

Journals

Comparative Education.
European Journal of Education.
International Journal of Early Childhood.

Variety 3: Multiple interrelated scenarios

A number of different types of problems related to one particular topic area. For example, a road traffic accident scene or a court scene.

Variety 4: Online games

For example, games that can be played in a multi-user virtual environment, such as Second Life. Games and simulations can increase students' motivation for learning and facilitate team building. In particular they are vital for team building in the initial stages of problem-based learning in virtual worlds.

Variety 5: Virtual patients

There are three distinct forms of virtual patient applications:

1   Computer simulations.
2   Electronic patient records.
3   Virtual patients for education: this is the form used for problem-based learning as these virtual patients include both the patients and their individual contexts.

Variety 6: Storyboard

Storyboards have been adapted from the film industry to business, and are used for planning. More recently the term 'storyboard' has been used in the fields of web and software development (Figure R.2).

Variety 7: Interaction or conversation analysis

This scenario is a written conversation that worked well facilitating students to generate ideas about characteristics of a leader, similarities and differences between male and female leaders, skills in managing tasks and leading personnel, responsibility for the work community, employees' well-being and

Figure R.2
Wee Angus.
From Wilke, K.
and Burns, I.,
Problem-based
Learning. A
Handbook for
Nurses, 2003.
Reproduced
with permission
of Palgrave
Macmillan.

the atmosphere. (Supplied by Pirjo Vuoskoski, Mikkeli University of Applied Sciences, Savonlinna Finland.)

Maija (nursing student, female) and Pekka (IT-specialist, male) are old friends. Here is a part of their mobile-phone discussion:

Pekka: ... I don't know why I am so tired all the time nowadays ...

Maija: Have you been very busy at work?

Pekka: Well, yeah ... we are all tired, because of the extra workload and working overtime ... our manager is always highlighting the importance of leisure time and social events, but there isn't really time for it ...

Maija: Don't you have any agreed office hours? Aren't there some laws regulating the daily working hours? What about your employment contract?

Pekka: Of course we have all those ... but nobody is looking at them, because the business is really going strong at the moment ... it is all about making the best possible profit at the moment ...

Maija: But I remember, when you started there ... It sounded such a good working place. And how they are advertising their human-oriented policy on their home page!

Pekka: Yeah, yeah ... there are all the values and mission statements of the organization, but I think nobody cares about them anymore ... we are all just working like crazy ... actually, our manager is doing the longest workdays!

Maija: I couldn't work like that ... At the hospitals I have been practicing, there has always been regular working hours and shifts. It's usually the head nurse, who makes the work shift lists, and all workers are expected to follow them ...

Pekka: ...well, I couldn't work like that ... at least we can always negotiate about our work time and responsibilities with our manager ... it is just a question, if he has time for us ...

Variety 8: Podcasts

Podcasts have become popular as students and teachers can share information and students can see or listen to lectures again. These can be made by staff, either as enhanced podcasts or voice only podcasts, or they can be downloaded and used from other sites. For example, the *Nature* podcast can be used in health, medicine and social care.

Variety 9: Picture collage

This scenario is a picture collage (see Figure R.3) that worked well facilitating students to generate ideas about the challenges of leadership and leaders' abilities to work as a manager of change, especially in the health care sector, emphasizing the domination of women, rapid technological development and richness in teamwork. (Supplied by Pirjo Vuoskoski, Mikkeli University of Applied Sciences, Savonlinna Finland.)

Figure R.3 Picture collage

Assessing PBLonline

Assessment in PBLonline requires no less thought and care than it does under other approaches to learning and teaching. However, the shifts in assessment practices since the early 2000s are rather worrying. Assessment in higher education is increasingly regulatory in nature and there seems to be an increasing desire to use such regulatory functions in online discussion forums. Yet over-regulation in discussion forums in PBLonline is likely to reduce team cohesion, effectiveness and the possibility for students to take responsibility for learning and developing independence in inquiry. Although Garrison and Anderson (2003) argue that 40–50 per cent of the course mark in online courses equates with participating in online discussion, it is not advisable to use such an approach when there are other options that better suit PBLonline. If we are to design assessment that fits with Constellations 7, 8 and 9 then it needs to be seen as developmental rather than regulatory, and as a practice that enables students to develop and come to an understanding of the literary practices of higher education and the disciplines in which they are studying. As Goodfellow and Lea (2005) point out:

> we cannot conflate the writing that students do in online discussion only with social or collaborative interaction but that the texts themselves are evidence of the different literacy practices through which students are constructing disciplinary knowledge.
>
> (Goodfellow and Lea, 2005: 267)

Further, Ulmer (2003a, 2003b) suggests that just transferring and transforming literacy onto the internet in the form of ready-made papers put on websites is not enough. Instead, he suggests that it is vital to create pedagogies that will enable the integration of internet practices with literate skills in new and innovative ways. Thus, he suggests the concept of 'electracy,' arguing that:

> what literacy is to the analytical mind, electracy is to the affective body: a prosthesis that enhances and augments a network of organic human

potential . . . If literacy focussed in universally valid methodologies of knowledge (sciences), electracy focuses on the individual state of mind within which knowing takes place (arts).

(Ulmer: 2003b)

In practice, what Ulmer suggests is that electracy should provide learners with:

- Information that is customizable.
- Opportunities to compose cognitive maps of their position within the field of collective knowledge (termed 'mystory', which comprises their story in the forms of a series of web pages of hypertextual compositions such as theorizing, images, symbols, links and personal narratives. The purpose of this activity is not only to learn how to create sites but also to record their learning and self-discovery through a biography).
- An opportunity to see writing as a selection of materials from archives.
- Assessment that is not exam driven, but instead focuses on improvisation, thus students are given a question and asked to do something with it.
- The ability to collaborate and be reflexive 'a promise and challenge of electrate education is to invent a pedagogy for group learning and self-knowledge'.

Much of what Ulmer is suggesting is the disruption of traditional ways of viewing learning and assessment, and interestingly he chooses to juxtapose science and arts. Yet what is missing from this is the necessity of engaging with discipline-based pedagogy and the complexity of managing assessment. Ulmer, in particular, seems to largely ignore the latter. Apart from arguing for the marrying of problem-based learning with electracy, it could be argued that what Ulmer is suggesting also has many similarities with Winter et al.'s patchwork text (Winter et al., 1999). This is a means of students presenting their work in written form. Students build up text in coursework over a number of weeks. Each component of work is shared with other students and they are expected to use different styles, for example, a commentary on a lecture, a personal account or a book review. The focus in the patchwork text is on creation, recreation, reflexivity, collaboration and self-story.

Thus it would seem that some forms of problem-based learning, mystory and patchwork text are all 'forms' of electracy or literacy that attempt to reconstitute text and subject. However, what Ulmer's electracy proposes that the others do not, is a clear setting out of the need to acknowledge and put into practice the notion that at the heart of learning is 'one's own being.' While the use of problem-based learning, patchwork text and action learning all locate the learner in a process, and acknowledge the importance of identity and identity shifts, these approaches are not as overt as mystory in terms of reflexive transformation.

Here are some of the possible assessment options for PBLonline:

Team presentation

Asking the students to submit their work orally (such as podcasts or voice-overs) or in written form as a collaborative piece, models the process of problem-based learning but is difficult to mark. Is content, process, presentation or a combination of these being marked?

Case-based individual essay

Here the student is presented with a case scenario that they respond to in the form of an essay. Students may be given a choice of scenarios from which to choose and the level of detail and complexity can vary from year to year. This links well with problem-based learning but still tends to focus largely on cognitive abilities (unless students are allowed to use narrative style essays). However, a link to their discussion postings (including their reflections on other peoples' postings) can enhance their essay and also illustrate the way in which the discussion forum has challenged and informed their thinking.

Case-based management plan related to clinical practice/client-led project

Here students are presented with a real life scenario to solve/manage for a client. One group of engineering students were given a bunch of coconuts and asked to design an effective tool to remove both the flesh and the milk. Another set of students were asked to resolve the difficulty of cracks occurring in railway lines crossing Central Australia caused by both excessive temperatures and train vibration. These are very effective but must be criterion-referenced, and therefore are disliked by some tutors and external examiners if the criteria are perceived to be too broad.

e-Portfolios

These can be unwieldy if not managed well and are difficult to mark. They are fine if they are well designed, but it seems that they are an area with which many academics struggle despite accessible software to support it such as PebblePad. Tosh *et al.* (2005) suggest a number of concerns that emerged from their findings such as:

- the need for buy-in by students;
- assessment practices;
- accessibility and technology;
- control over access;
- motivation.

McAlpine (2005: 382) states 'The narrative aspects of 'e-portfolios as story' suggest a self-constructed identity portrayed through the e-portfolio' yet it is not entirely clear how this differs from how one portrays one's self in temporal portfolios (seems a better description than non e-portfolios). Further, she argues:

> There is also a difference between the narrative identity embodied in the individuals as described by Ricoeur and the narrative identity embodied in the portfolio. In an individual the power to recast stories remains within the individual, who is free to reshape actions in the light of reflection, to construct new plots which over-power the old, and present them in a new temporal framework. However, in portfolios, the process of emplotment is laid bare through the reflective comments and feedback that is presented, as the power over temporal structuring is undermined by database structure, which affords equal value given to all entries.
>
> (McAlpine, 2005: 383)

Yet recasting stories, constructing plots and new plots is also true of temporal portfolios. Surely too the extent to which one allows the database to order and privilege for ones self is a matter of choice, creativity and structure, and choice of tool. There are also arguments by McAlpine that the e-portfolio becomes a virtual identity – yet it is not clear how this is different (or the same) as the identities that are presented in discussion boards and blogs.

Online journals

These have worked well in engineering and health. Students hand them in each week and receive a mark at the end of each term/semester. Students tend to be more open and honest about their learning than one would expect and these can be criterion-referenced.

Team wikis

These work well with PBLonline and can also be used successfully in terms of a team writeboard. Team wikis allow multiple users to contribute to a website, essentially web pages that are editable by a number of people. What is also useful about these is that it is possible to assess who has contributed what to the wiki and the collaborative work. However, as in collaborative assessment, it is important to award a team mark so that the team learns to manage the passengers, lurkers and thinkers. Further as Lea (2001) pointed out:

> Collaborative learning is not just about enabling a dialogue between students working together, and pooling their understandings of authori-

tative published works; it can also be about creating collaborative texts
. . . even when the final piece of work is that of an individual student for
assessment purposes.

(Lea, 2001: 178)

Blogs

Weblogs have become a popular web-publishing form in the last 2 or 3 years,
and are perhaps best described as web-based diaries where students use them
as online reflective diaries, a space – a place to bring together reflections,
thoughts and ideas. Blogs are invariably assessed on issues such as:

* *Reflection*: The extent to which the blog illustrates criticality and
  reflection through the period of the course or module.
* *Regularity*: The extent to which blog entries are frequent and substantial,
  spread throughout the course.
* *Knowledge and understanding*: This section of the blog should demonstrate in-depth understanding of the area under study and the ability to
  take a critical stance towards the knowledge and perspectives being
  offered through the course.

Hamish Macleod at the University of Edinburgh suggests:

> . . . the weblog is the place to reflect on the theoretical and experiential
> issues that you believe to be important, the review exercise invites you
> to analyse an extant example of practice, and the design exercise gives
> you an opportunity to design and (perhaps) build something for yourself.
> In all cases however, the subject matter can be decided by your free
> choice. Ideally, topics would be chosen that were directly relevant to your
> own practice, or personal development. One way to approach this would
> be to consider developing game-informed approaches for work with
> your own students, and in your own subject area. Remember, and be
> assured, that a successful piece of work may be one which explores some
> avenues and comes to the conclusion that this or that approach would be
> unlikely to prove successful for your purposes. Research has been defined
> as the business of going up alleys to see whether they are blind.

Hypertext essays

These are scholarly works or artifacts that can only be realized electronically
and have been written with particular hypertext practices in mind. These
include, for example, multilinearity, repetition, mixed media and multivocality. A hypertext essay can be read in many different ways. McKenna
and McAvinia (2007) suggest 'when it comes to analyzing hypertext writing,

there has been much written by theorists about fiction and professional, published, academic writing ... however, there has been rather less said about how student writers are experimenting with academic hypertext'. They suggest that hypertext writing might subvert the dominant forms of meaning-making in higher education, further the students in their study suggested that hypertext writing did both appear to be and challenge them to operate within a different form of academic discourse than more traditional forms of essay writing.

Patchwork text

This is a way of getting students to present their work in written form. Students build up text in coursework over a number of weeks. Each component of work is shared with other students and they are expected to use different styles, such as a commentary on a lecture, a personal account or a book review. This kind of assessment fits well with problem-based learning because of its emphasis on critique and self-questioning. (See R. Winter *et al.*, 1999.)

Peer assessment

This involves students making judgments about other students' work, either by using their own assessment criteria or that provided by tutors, which can sometimes be better. This kind of assessment emphasizes the co-operative nature of PBLonline and McConnell (2006) offers a detailed and practical use of peer and collaborative assessment in several chapters of his book. However, inter and intra-peer assessment is also useful:

* *Inter-peer assessment* – students from one problem-based learning team assess the work of another team.
* *Intra-peer assessment* – students assess the product of what they themselves have produced as a team.

E-valuating PBLonline

To evaluate something is to determine or fix the value of it. While many see evaluation as determining significance, worth, or condition of changes in behaviour, performance and competencies, rather I hold the view that you should *assess people* and *evaluate things*. In the case of problem-based learning, we believe we should assess students and facilitators, but we should evaluate problem-based learning programmes. Therefore, evaluation is defined as something undertaken to determine the effectiveness of programmes and projects designed to produce change, which is carried out by careful appraisal and study.

This section will suggest ways of undertaking evaluations of problem-based learning online. It will suggest that evaluation needs to explore problem-based learning online from a number of perspectives and it will also suggest which forms of evaluation fit best with problem-based learning online.

Authors such as Crawley (1999) and Britain and Liber (2004) have advocated the use of Laurillard's conversational model (Laurillard, 1993), as a means of evaluating virtual learning environments, since it can be used to examine constructivist and conversational approaches to learning. This model contains key characteristics that mirror some of the processes involved in problem-based learning:

Discursive – teachers' and learners' conceptions are accessible to each other, they agree learning goals for the topic and students receive feedback on discussion related to the topic goal

Adaptive – the teacher uses the relationship between their own and the students' conceptions to guide the dialogue

Interactive – the students take responsibility for achieving the goal and the teacher provides feedback on the actions

Reflective – the teacher supports the process whereby students link the feedback on their actions to the topic goal for each level of description within the structure of the topic

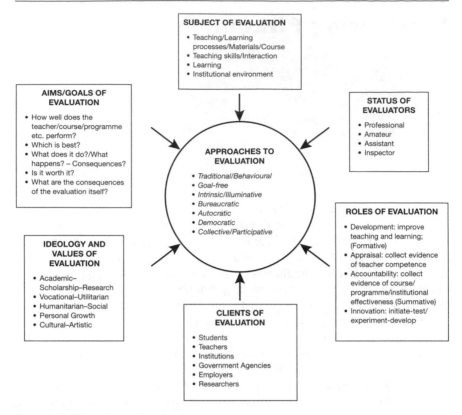

Figure R.4 Dimensions of evaluation
Source: Adapted from Cox *et al.* (1981)

Although this model has considerable use as a device for evaluating computer mediated problem-based learning, it is problematic for two reasons. First, the focus is largely on teacher guidance and direction, rather than developing student autonomy and peer discussion. Second, it only really deals with interactions between a single student and a teacher, and thus omits peer group interaction and the tools required by the teacher to facilitate a number of students (Figure R.4).

Models of evaluation that fit with PBLonline

Evaluation models all have distinct purposes and uses, some of which are more appropriate for problem-based learning than others. Perhaps a more useful way would be to combine Laurillard's model with that of Cox *et al.* (1981), who suggest a number of styles and dimensions of evaluation. However, I suggest the following approaches to evaluation are some of the ones that fit well with PBLonline.

Naturalistic evaluation

This model (Lincoln and Guba, 1985) involves gathering descriptive information regarding the evaluation object, setting, surrounding conditions, relevant issues, and values and standards for worth and merit; determining information desired by and sharing with relevant audiences; and negotiating decisions. This model, with its focus on collaboration and negotiation, is perhaps the one most useful for PBLonline when exploring users' and students' experience, because it involves collaboration with participants and is based upon their lived experiences.

Illuminative evaluation

This increases understanding and describes programmes. It focuses on the actual learning situation or the learning milieu (Parlett and Dearden, 1977) and is conducted in three overlapping stages of observing, inquiring and then seeking explanations. This method can increase our knowledge of the issues connected with the types of problems used, contexts in which PBLonline has been implemented and facilitator–student dynamics. Illuminative evaluation involves study of a programme or part of a programme and the evaluator's task is to provide an understanding of new innovation by:

- becoming familiar with the day-to-day realities of the settings being studied;
- explaining observed patterns and cause-and-effect relationships.

Data collection in PBLonline may therefore involve

- collecting information that can be used in the development of user support;
- collection of information for the evaluation of efficiency/effectiveness of investments;
- evaluation of coherence between technical and educational goals.

Goal free evaluation

This describes programmes and focuses on improvement; Scriven (1972) suggests that it occurs when evaluators are not cued to the programme's goals. Scriven's model has some interesting implications for PBLonline programmes that have overt goals that drive programme development, such as Constellations 1 and 2.

The countenance model

Best described by Stake (1978), this model is descriptive in nature and looks at prior conditions or antecedents; implementation or transactions;

and outcomes. It is in keeping with Astin's I-E-O model: inputs, environment, outcomes (Astin, 1993). It has some usefulness in PBLonline when evaluators want to know what outcomes are related directly to the experience.

The Context, Inputs, Process, Products (CIPP) model

This was described by Stufflebeam (2000), is again descriptive, and focuses on describing programme goals, design, implementation and outcomes. This model has more relevance to problem-based learning as it focuses on process and acknowledges context, but will only be useful for some constellations of PBLonline, such as Constellations 1, 2 and 3.

Action research

There are various approaches in the world of action research, but the focus of this section is on participatory action research. Many of the early forms of action research combined qualitative and quantitative approaches and focused on clear goals and steps. Action research was largely seen as the analysis of a situation in order to improve it (Elliott, 1991). Thus the aims are to improve practice and the understanding of practice through a combination of systematic reflection and strategic innovation to improve practice rather than to produce knowledge. It involves a series of steps as presented in Table R.1. This approach can be used across all constellations of PBLonline. However, for Constellations 7, 8 and 9, participatory action research will be more appropriate since this involves examining an issue systematically from the perspectives and lived experiences of the community members most affected. Due to the participatory nature of the process, PAR seeks to bring about empowering benefits. This method of research is thus often associated with social transformation in the developing world and human rights activism (Kemmis and McTaggart, 2005).

Appreciative inquiry

Appreciative inquiry was developed by Cooperrider and Srivastva in the 1980s (Cooperrider and Srivastva, 1987). This approach is based on the premise that 'organizations change in the direction in which they inquire' and has roots in both action research and organizational development. The research is directed towards appreciating what it is about the social world, project or organization that is positive, and exploring this. However, since its inception it has been adapted for use in higher education where the focus is on four stages, termed the 4D model:

• *Discover* – those involved in the change or project discuss what was best, what was positive, invariably using semi-structured interviews.

- *Dream* – people are asked to remember and envisage peak moments discovered in the 'discover' phase and try to see them as the norm rather than the exceptional.
- *Design* – a team or a series of small teams are then asked to go and design ways of creating the 'dream' situation.
- *Destiny* – the final phase is to implement the changes.

This approach is increasingly being used in large online evaluation, certainly in the UK, with much of the work in this area being promoted by Rhona Sharpe at Oxford Brookes University, UK.

Table R.1 The action research cycle

Identifying and clarifying the original idea

The 'general idea' refers to a state of affairs or situation one wishes to change or improve upon. For example, students are dissatisfied with the methods by which they are assessed. How can we collaborate to improve student assessment?

Reconnaissance

1 Describing the facts of the situation: Who is dissatisfied? What are they dissatisfied with?

2 Explaining the facts of the situation: How does this arise? What are the critical factors which have a bearing on the state of affairs?

Constructing the general plan

1 A revised statement of the general idea – which will have changed by now

2 A statement of factors one is going to change: for example, modifying the way that assessments are presented to students

3 A statement of negotiations one had or will have before undertaking the proposed course of action, for example, discuss with staff and students

4 A statement of required resources, for example, materials, equipment

5 A statement of the ethical framework which will govern access to and release of information

Developing next action steps

Decide exactly which courses of action in the general plan must be undertaken next and how the process of implementation and its effects are going to be monitored.

Implementing next action steps

It may take some time to implement a course of action – it usually implies changes in all the participants' behaviour.

Source: Adapted from Elliott, 1991.

However, perhaps one of the most recent approaches to evaluation is that provided by van Frans Ronteltap at the University of Maastricht, who suggests PBLonline might be considered through the following perspectives. It is a model that can be used with appreciative inquiry or action research.

1   *Technical perspective*:
    a   Integration of tools and applications in the learning environment of participating institutions.
    b   Functionality of the tools for use in problem-based learning.

2   *Organizational perspective*:
    a   Relevant knowledge and skills of academics for development and assessment of teaching and learning.
    b   Acceptance and user satisfaction of the tools.

3   *Pedagogical perspective*:
    a   Content and structure of the courses.
    b   Coherence of technology in use and pedagogical principles.

Frequently asked questions

Why use PBLonline?

While some staff might see PBLonline being adopted because of timetabling and difficulties with large cohorts, most people implement PBLonline because they want to help students equip themselves with the experience of, and capabilities for, online learning. However, there is also a sense that PBLonline might offer more flexibility for students and provide opportunities to use liquid learning and student-centred produsage, rather than covering content and just using VLEs as knowledge repositories.

How do I get started?

The key to developing effective PBLonline is to focus on what you want students to learn, plan the module/programme well and in good time, and ensure that the problem scenarios are well designed and tested before implementation. One useful means of getting started is to facilitate PBLonline with someone who is experienced and can provide mentoring. A further alternative is to gain access to several PBLonline programmes and evaluate what has been implemented that you might be able to use to inform your own programme.

What do students think about it?

Most students enjoy the challenge of PBLonline and in particular value the flexibility it offers. For many students content management systems and portals built specifically for PBLonline have been useful. Many of the complaints voiced by students relate to poor course organization, difficulty with the technology and concerns with peers who both lurk and over-engage.

Is facilitating PBLonline very different from face-to-face facilitation?

In some ways there are many similarities and in other ways there are not. For many staff, new to facilitation online, the difficulties they experience relate to not being able to 'read' students because of the lack of visual cues, although many gain skills in understanding online tone over a period of time. A further issue that emerges for staff is knowing how much to 'moderate' or 'facilitate'; some experienced face-to-face facilitators tend to say little online and at the outset students tend to need guidance. On the other hand those inexperienced in online moderation may intervene too much, thereby preventing student ownership of the team work.

What are the most important design principles for PBLonline?

There needs to be a real clarity about how the course and the scenarios are created so that they produce robust educational discussion, but the main design issues are discussed in Chapter 5. The main principles are:

1   Focus on what it is you want students to learn – not content coverage.
2   Decide how this learning will be assessed.
3   Decide how you expect them to learn.

Is PBLonline better blended with face-to-face learning or better fully online?

Although it could be argued that distance courses have different functions from face-to-face ones, and that the students undertaking them have different motivations from those studying on face-to-face programmes, much of the success of PBLonline depends on the way it is planned, designed and implemented. To date there is little research that suggests that one approach is better or worse than another.

Do students have to meet face-to-face first for PBLonline to work?

The whole issue of whether it is important to meet first in order for PBLonline to work is contested ground. Many staff I have spoken with who have undertaken research into online learning (though not PBLonline) suggest that it is vital. Other staff disagree. I believe that it is unnecessary for students to meet first in order to work as an effective team, but I do believe that it is vital for students to undergo team building and preparation for PBLonline before the course commences.

Where is it being used?

PBLonline is being used worldwide in a variety of disciplines. Currently most staff are using it in blended modules rather than adopting a cross programme approach, although there are several PBLonline distance programmes and a number of blended programmes under development.

What are the biggest difficulties with it?

The biggest difficulties seem to be in ensuring that staff and students feel equipped to undertake PBLonline and then able to participate. Non-participation by students and poor engagement by staff usually emerges because they feel uneasy with the approach, frightened of the technology and ill-equipped to participate.

Does it cost more?

It is perhaps more expensive in terms of both staff and students' time at the outset of the programme, but it seems to be no less expensive than other forms of learning. The cost of Second Life Islands, new software and educating staff to undertake PBLonline tend to be high initial start-up costs, but then this would seem to be the case with most innovations. In the end it depends whether costs are related to use of staff time, course effectiveness or quality of the learning and facilitation.

What happens if students don't participate?

This depends on what is meant by participation – often what staff mean relates to wanting students to participate in particular ways for particular purposes. However, student experiences indicate that while they may not be participating in the discussion forum, they may be meeting in other ways or undertaking tasks that tutors do not know about (see for example, the discussion earlier in Chapter 4). Before accusing students of not participating it is better to find out first just what they *are* doing. Assessing the discussion board postings does little really to alleviate this, so it is best to try to encourage students to develop their own ground rules and build the team well at the outset. Team assessment does help to ensure participation in the team activities but these need to be well designed too.

Glossary

Avatar the bodily manifestation of one's self in the context of a 3D virtual world.

Blogs (weblogs) personal websites consisting of regularly updated entries displayed in reverse chronological order. They may be used by learners in PBLonline to evidence their thinking openly to the rest of the team and the e-tutor.

Bumping an aggressive act in Second Life of purposefully bumping into another avatar.

Commodification the turning of an object into a commodity, where it has some exchange value, other than the effort taken in its production. With the wider reader audience offered by technology, students find a value for their writing that goes beyond the grade.

Community of practice a group of professionals informally bound to one another through exposure to common problems and common pursuit of solutions, thereby generating within themselves a body of 'expert' knowledge.

Constructionism this learning philosophy states that learning is best when the learner is engaged in an active role of designer and constructor, especially where the learner is consciously engaged in constructing something that will be shared, for example, with other members of a virtual team.

Constructivism this learning theory is based on the concept that knowledge is created by the learner based on mental activity. Conceptual growth comes from sharing individual constructions and changing perceptions in response to the perceptions of others. Learning is best situated in an environment reflective of real world contexts (Piaget, 1954).

Cyberspace currently used to describe the whole range of information resources available through computer networks.

Dialogic learning   learning that occurs when insights and understandings emerge through dialogue in a learning environment. It is a form of learning where students draw upon their own experience to explain the concepts and ideas with which they are presented, and then use that experience to make sense for themselves and also to explore further issues.

Dialogic spaces   spaces that transcend conceptions of dialogue (conceived as the notion of exchange of ideas) and dialectic (conceived as the notion of transformation through contestability). Dialogic spaces also encompass the complex relationship that occurs between oral and written communication and the way, in particular, that written communication is understood by the reader.

Digital spaces   those spaces in which communication and interaction are assisted, created or enhanced by digital media.

Disjunction   a sense of fragmentation of part of, or all of the self, characterized by frustration and confusion, and a loss of sense of self, which often results in anger and the need for right answers.

Electracy   the creation of pedagogies that will enable the integration of internet practices with literate skills in new and innovative ways.

E-portfolio   a collection of electronic evidence such as Word and PDF files, images, multimedia, blog entries and Web links assembled and managed by a student, often online.

Frame factors   issues that are raised by students that do not directly relate to the problem scenario. For example, transport between campuses, the arrival of student uniforms or students' personal problems.

Generation CX   while 'Generation C' is being used to capture the idea that we live in an age of content producers, Generation CX is being used to include not just content but context, Cook (2007).

Generation X   those born in the period of the 1960s–1975.

Generation Y   those born in the period of the 1970s–1990s.

Hypertext   writing on the web that incorporates the use of hyperlinks.

Hypertext essay   scholarly work or artifact that can only be realized electronically and has been written with particular hypertext practices in mind. This includes, for example, multilinearity, repetition, mixed media and multivocality. A hypertext essay can be read in many different ways.

Jumping   a way of greeting someone in Second Life by making one's avatar jump.

Knowledge repository   reflects the idea that many programmes still use VLEs as places to deposit large amounts of 'knowledge' that students are supposed to cover.

Learning context   the interplay of all the values, beliefs, relationships, frameworks and external structures that operate within a given learning environment.

Learner identity   an identity formulated through the interaction of learner and learning. The notion of learner identity moves beyond, but encapsulates the notion of learning style, and encompasses positions that students take up in learning situations, whether consciously or unconsciously.

Learning stances   the three stances (personal, pedagogical and inter-actional) that together form the framework of Dimensions of Learner Experience.

Liminality   characterized by a stripping away of old identities and an oscil-lation between states, it is a betwixt and between state and there is a sense of being in a period of transition, often on the way to a new or different space.

Liquid Learning   characterized by emancipation, reflexivity and flexibility, so that knowledge and knowledge boundaries are contestable and always on the move.

Lurking   a person who reads chatroom discussions, group or message board postings, but does not contribute.

Managed learning environment (MLE)   a software system designed to assist teachers in managing online educational programmes. It includes access control, e-learning content, communication tools and the adminis-tration of user groups.

Mobile learning   defined as learning for learners on the move and is based on the assumption that considerable learning takes place not only outside the calssroom, but also that people create sites for learning within their surroundings.

Mode 1 knowledge (Gibbons *et al.*, 1994)   propositional knowledge that is produced within the academe separate from its use. The academe is considered the traditional environment for the generation of Mode 1 knowledge.

Mode 2 knowledge (Gibbons *et al.*, 1994)   knowledge that transcends disciplines and is produced in, and validated through the world of work. Knowing in this mode demands the integration of skills and abilities in order to act in a particular context.

Moodle a free software e-learning platform designed to help educators create online courses. Its open source license and modular design allows for global development.

Net generation the generation that has barely known a world without computers, the World Wide Web, highly interactive video games and mobile phones. For many of this generation instant messaging, rather than telephone or email, is the primary form of communication.

Online tone hearing what is being 'said' in an online context, particularly in discussion forums, and being able to locate anger, distress and pleasure, without the use of emoticons. The ability to 'read' voices is something that needs to be developed by facilitators.

PebblePad an e-Portfolio system that allows users to build and develop artifacts related to their studies.

Pedagogical stance the way in which people see themselves as learners in particular educational environments.

Performativity the increasing focus in higher education on what students are able to *do*, which has emerged from the desire to equip students for life and work. Higher education is sliding towards encouraging students to perform rather than to necessarily critique and do.

Personal stance the way in which staff and students see themselves in relation to the learning context and give their own distinctive meaning to their experience of that context.

Podcast a digital media file, or a series of such files, that is distributed over the Internet.

Posting (verb) to publish a message on an online forum or discussion group; (noun) a message published on an online forum or discussion group.

Problem-based learning an approach to learning where the focus for learning is on problem situations, rather than content. Students work in small teams and are facilitated by a tutor.

Problem-based learning team a number of students (four to ten) who work together as a defined group.

Problem-solving learning teaching where the focus is on students solving a given problem by acquiring the answers expected by the lecturer, answers that are rooted in the information supplied in some way to the students. The solutions are bounded by the content and students are expected to explore little extra material other than that with which they have been provided, in order to discover the solutions.

Problem-based learning online   a generic term that captures that vast variety of ways in which problem-based learning is being used synchronously and asynchronously, on campus, or at a distance. It represents the idea that students learn through web-based materials including text, simulations, videos and demonstrations, and resources such as chatrooms, message boards and environments that have been purpose-built for problem-based learning.

Produsage   artifacts developed by a community (Bruns, 2007). Produsage projects are continually under development, and therefore always unfinished; their development is evolutionary, and iterative.

Scaffolding   the concept of scaffolding is based on Vygotsky's zone of proximal development (Vygotsky, 1978). Individualized support designed to facilitate a student's ability to build on prior knowledge and to generate and internalize new knowledge is provided by the tutor or other students. The support is pitched just beyond the current level of the student.

Screenager   member of a younger generation of students who have found, through their engagement with new digital technologies, a means of thriving in environments of uncertainty and complexity.

Second Life   a 3D virtual world created by LindenLab set in an internet-based world. Residents (in the forms of self-designed avatars) in this world interact with each other and can learn, socialize, participate in activities, and buy and sell items with one another.

Sloodle   a blending of Second Life and Moodle, which allows students to post blog entries directly from Second Life.

Smooth spaces   open, flexible and contested spaces in which both learning and learners are always on the move. Students here would be encouraged to contest knowledge and ideas proffered by the lecturers and in so doing create their own stance toward knowledge(s).

Stance   one's attitude, belief or disposition towards a particular context, person or experience. It refers to a particular position one takes up in life towards something, at a particular point in time.

Striated spaces   spaces characterized by a strong sense of organization and boundedness. Learning in such spaces is epitomized though course attendance, and defined learning places such as lecture theatres and classrooms.

Radio button   a circular hole on websites that contains either white space for unselected or a dot for selected.

Reflective spaces spaces in which our constructions of reality are no longer reinforced by the forces of our socio-cultural world, so that we begin to move from a state or position of reflection into reflective spaces.

Threshold concept the idea of a portal that opens up a way of thinking that was previously inaccessible (Meyer and Land, 2003).

Transition shifts in learner experience caused by a challenge to the person's life-world. Transitions occur in particular areas of students' lives, at different times and in distinct ways. The notion of transitions carries with it the idea of movement from one place to another and with it the necessity of taking up a new position in a different place.

Transitional learning learning that occurs as a result of critical reflection upon shifts (transitions) that have taken place for the students personally (including viscerally), pedagogically and/or interactionally.

Troublesome spaces places where 'stuckness' or 'disjunction' occurs.

Troublesome knowledge Perkins (1999) described conceptually difficult knowledge as 'troublesome knowledge'. This is knowledge that appears, for example, counter intuitive, alien (emanating from another culture or discourse), or incoherent (discrete aspects are unproblematic but there is no organizing principle).

Virtual learning environment (VLE) a set of learning and teaching tools involving online technology designed to enhance students' learning experience, for example, Blackboard, WebCT.

Virtual patients simulations or representations of individuals who are designed by facilitators as a means of creating a character in a health care setting.

Wilfing a term used to describe browsing the internet with no specific purpose. It is aimless surfing which seems to partly have emerged from starting to look for something and then becoming side-tracked. The term is an acronym for 'what was I looking for?' hence WILF.

Wikis server software that allows multiple users to contribute to, and edit web page content.

References

Alexander, B. (2006) Web 2.0: a new wave of innovation for teaching and learning?, *Educause Review*, 41(2): www.educause.edu/apps/er/erm06/erm0621.asp. Accessed 26 October 2006.

Almy, T.P., Colby, K.K., Zubkoff, M., Gephart, D.S., Moore-West, M. and Lundquist, L.L. (1992) Health, society and the physician: problem-based learning of the social sciences and humanities, *Annals of Internal Medicine*, 116(7): 569–574.

Astin, A.W. (1993) *What Matters in College: Four Critical Years Revisited*. San Francisco, California: Jossey-Bass.

Barrows, H.S. (1986) A taxonomy of problem-based learning methods, *Medical Education*, 20(6): 481–486.

Barrows, H.S. (2000) *Problem-based Learning Applied to Medical Education*. Springfield, Illinois: Southern Illinois University Press.

Barrows, H.S. (2002) Is it truly possible to have such a thing as dPBL? *Distance Education*, 23(1): 119–122.

Barrows, H.S. and Tamblyn, R.M. (1980) *Problem-based Learning: An Approach to Medical Education*. New York: Springer Publishing.

Bauman, Z. (2000) *Liquid Modernity*. Cambridge: Polity Press.

Bayne, S. (2005a) 'Deceit, desire and control: the identities of learners and teachers in cyberspace', in R. Land and S. Bayne (eds) *Education in Cyberspace*, 26–41. London: Routledge.

Bayne, S. (2005b) 'Higher education as a visual practice: seeing though the virtual learning environment'. Paper presented to annual conference of the Society for Research into Higher Education, 13–15 December 2005, the University of Edinburgh, Scotland. Available at www.malts.ed.ac.uk/staff/sian/visualpractice.pdf. Accessed 10 October 2007.

Beaumont, C. and Chew, C.S. (2006) 'Analysing the use of communication tools for collaboration in problem-based learning online', in M. Savin-Baden and K. Wilkie (eds) *Problem-based Learning Online*, 191–209. Maidenhead: McGraw Hill.

Berg, B. and Östergren, B. (1979) Innovation processes in higher education, *Studies in Higher Education*, 4(2): 261–269.

Bodington Open Source Project. Available at: http://bodington.org/index.php. Accessed 6 December 2006.

Boettcher, J.V. and Conrad, R.M. (1999) *Faculty Guide for Moving Teaching and Learning to the Web*. Mission Viejo, California: League for Innovation in the Community College.

Boud, D. (ed.) (1985) *Problem-based Learning in Education for the Professions.* Sydney: Higher Education Research and Development Society of Australasia.

Boud, D. and Feletti, G. (1997) 'Changing problem-based learning: introduction to second edition', in D. Boud and G. Feletti (eds) *The Challenge of Problem Based Learning* (2nd edition), 14–20. London: Kogan Page.

Boud, D. and Miller, N. (eds) (1996) *Working with Experience: Animating Learning.* London: Routledge.

Bridges, E.M. and Hallinger, P. (1996) 'Problem-based learning in leadership education', in L. Wilkerson and W.H. Gijselaers (eds) *New Directions for Teaching and Learning*, 53–61. San Francisco, California: Jossey-Bass.

Britain, S. and Liber, O. (2004) 'A framework for the pedagogical evaluation of e-learning environments'. Report to JISC Technology Applications Programme. Available at: www.cetis.ac.uk/members/pedagogy/files/4thMeet_framework/ VLEfullReport. Accessed 28 July 2006.

Bruns, A. (2007) 'Beyond difference: reconfiguring education for the user-led age'. Paper presented at Ideas in Cyberspace Education 3, Ross Priory, Loch Lomond, 21–23 March. Available at: www.education.ed.ac.uk/ice3/papers/bruns.html.

Casey, M.B. and Howson, P. (1993) Educating preservice students based on a problem-centered approach to teaching, *Journal of Teacher Education*, 44(5): 1–9.

Carlson, L. (1989) 'Effective moderation of computer conferences: hints for moderators', in M.G. Brochet (ed.) *Moderating Conferences*, 6.10–16.13. Guelph, Ontario: University of Guelph.

Collis, B. (1997) Pedagogical reengineering: a pedagogical approach to course enrichment and redesign with the WWW, *Educational Technology Review*, 8: 11–15.

Collison, G., Elbaum, B., Haavind, S. and Tinker, R. (2000) *Facilitating Online Learning: Effective Strategies for Moderators.* Madison, Wisconsin: Atwood Publishing.

Conway, J. and Little, P. (2000) Adopting PBL as the preferred institutional approach to teaching and learning: considerations and challenges, *Journal on Excellence in College Teaching*, 11(2/3): 11–26.

Cook, J. (2007) 'Smells like teen spirit: Generation CX'. Paper presented at Ideas in Cyberspace Education 3, Ross Priory, Loch Lomond, 21–23 March. Available at: www.education.ed.ac.uk/ice3/papers/cook.html.

Cooperrider, D.L. and Srivastva, S. (1987) 'Appreciative inquiry in organizational life', in W. Pasmore and R. Woodman (eds) *Research in Organization Change and Development*, 129–169. Greenwich, Connecticut: JAI Press (Volume 1).

Cordeiro, P. and Campbell, B. (1996) 'Increasing the transfer of learning through problem-based learning in educational administration'. ERIC Document Reproduction Service No. ED 396 434.

Cox, R., Kontianen, S., Rea, N. and Robinson, S. (1981) *Learning and Teaching: An Evaluation of a Course for Teachers in General Practice.* London: University Teaching Methods Unit, Institute of Education.

Crawley, R.M. (1999) Evaluating CSCL – Theorists' and Users' Perspectives. Available at: www.bton.ac.uk/cscl/jtap/paper1.htm. Accessed 8 November 2005.

de Graaff, E. and Kolmos, A. (2003) Characteristics of problem-based learning, *International Journal of Engineering Education*, 19(5): 657–662.

Donnelly, R. (2006) 'The academic developer as tutor in PBLonline in higher education', in M. Savin-Baden and K. Wilkie (eds) *Problem-based Learning Online*, 79–97. Maidenhead: McGraw Hill.

Duch, B., Groh, S. and Allen, D. (eds) (2001) *The Power of Problem-based Learning*. Sterling, Virginia: Stylus.

Ebenezer, C. (1993) User Survey Conducted at the Medical Library of the University of Limburg at Maastricht. Technical Report, Medical Library, University of Limburg. Available at: http://dlist.sir.arizona.edu/archive/00000242/. Accessed 15 September 2003.

Ellaway, R., Dewhurst, D. and Cromar, S. (2004) Challenging the Mortality of Computer Assisted Learning Materials in the Life Sciences: The RECAL Project, Bioscience Education E-Journal. Available at: http://bio.ltsn.ac.uk/journal/vol3/beej-3-7.htm. Accessed 23 May 2007.

Elliott, J. (1991) *Action Research for Educational Change*. Buckingham: Open University Press.

Elton, L. (1996) Task differentiation in universities. Towards a new collegiality, *Tertiary Education and Management*, 2(2): 138–145.

Feenberg, A. (1989) 'The written world: on the theory and practice of computer conferencing', in R. Mason and A. Kaye (eds) *Mindweave: Communication, Computers and Distance Education*, 22–39. Elmsford, NY: Pergamon Press.

Freire, P. (1972) *Pedagogy of the Oppressed*. London: Penguin Books.

Freire, P. (1974) *Education: The Practice of Freedom*. London: Writers and Readers Co-operative.

Garrison, D.R. and Anderson, T. (2003) *eLearning in the Twenty-First Century*. London: RoutledgeFalmer.

Gibbons, M., Limoges, C., Nowotny, H., Schwarzman, S., Scott, P. and Trow, M. (1994) *The New Production of Knowledge: The Dynamics of Science and Research in Contemporary Societies*. London: Sage.

Goodfellow, R. and Lea, M. (2005) Supporting writing for assessment in online learning, *Assessment and Evaluation in Higher Education*, 30(3): 261–271.

Henri, F. and Rigault, C. (1996) 'Collaborative distance education and computer conferencing', in T. Liao (ed.) *Advanced Educational Technology: Research Issues and Future Potential*, 45–76. Berlin: Springer-Verlag.

Heron, J. (1989) *The Facilitator's Handbook*. London: Kogan Page.

Heron, J. (1993) *Group Facilitation*. London: Kogan Page.

Hmelo-Silver, C.E., Nagarajan, A. and Derry, S.J. (2006) 'From face-to-face to online participation: tensions in facilitating problem-based learning', in M. Savin-Baden and K. Wilkie (eds) *Problem-based Learning Online*, 61–78. Maidenhead: McGraw Hill.

Holmes, D.B. and Kaufman, D.M. (1994) Tutoring in problem-based learning: a teacher developmental process, *Medical Education*, 28(4): 275–283.

hooks, b. (1994) *Teaching to Transgress*. London: Routledge.

Jacques, D. (2000) *Learning in Groups*, (2nd edition). London: Croom Helm.

Jewitt, C. (2005) Multimodality, "reading" and "writing" for the twenty-first century, *Discourse: Studies in the Cultural Politics of Education*, 26(3): 315–331.

Johnson, D.W., Johnson, R.T. and Smith, K.A. (1991) 'Cooperative learning: increasing college faculty instructional productivity'. ASHE-ERIC Higher Education Report 4. Washington, DC: The George Washington University, School of Education and Social Development.

Johnson, D.W., Johnson, R.T. and Smith, K.A. (1998) *Active Learning: Cooperation in the College Collaborative Learning Classroom.* Edina, Minnesota: Interaction Book Company.

Jones, G., Miller, S., England, M. and Bilham, T. (2006) 'Virtual clinics: online places for problem-based learning', *ALT Newsletter*, Issue 4, April. Available at http:// newsletter.alt.ac.uk/e_article000562790.cfm?x=b11,0,w. Accessed 10 October 2007.

Kane, P. (2005) *The Play Ethic: A Manifesto for a Different Way of Living.* London: Pan.

Karmel, P. (1973) 'Expansion of medical education: report of the committee on medical schools to the Australian Universities Commission'. Canberra: Australian Government Publishing Service (AGPS).

Kaye, A.R. (1992) 'Learning together apart', in A.R. Kaye (ed.) *Collaborative Learning Through Computer Conferencing*, 1–24. London: Springer-Verlag.

Koschmann, T., Kelson, A.C., Feltovich, P.J. and Barrows, H.S. (1996) 'Computer-supported problem-based learning: a principled approach to the use of computers in collaborative learning', in T.D. Koschmann (ed.) *CSCL: Theory and Practice of an Emerging Paradigm*, 83–124. Mahwah, New Jersey: Lawrence Erlbaum.

Kress, G. (2007) 'Culture, technology and (environments of) learning'. Keynote speech presented at Ideas in Cyberspace Education 3, Ross Priory, Loch Lomond, 21–23 March.

Land, R. and Bayne, S. (2005) 'Screen or monitor? Issues of surveillance and disciplinary power in online learning environments', in R. Land and S. Bayne (eds) *Education in Cyberspace*, 165–178. London: RoutledgeFalmer.

Laurillard, D. (1993) *Rethinking University Teaching – A Framework for the Effective Use of Educational Technology.* London: Routledge.

Lea, M. (2001) Computer conferencing and assessment: new ways of writing in higher education, *Studies in Higher Education*, 26(2): 163–181.

Lee, K. (2006) 'Developing expertise in professional practice, online, at a distance', in M. Savin-Baden and K. Wilkie (eds) *Problem-based Learning Online*, 140–154. Maidenhead: McGraw Hill.

Lincoln, Y.S. and Guba, E.G. (1985) *Naturalistic Inquiry.* Beverly Hills, California: Sage Publishing.

Luck, P. and Norton, B. (2004) Problem based management learning-better online? *European Journal of Open and Distance Learning*, 2004/II: www.eurodl.org/ materials/contrib/2004/Luck_Norton.htm. Accessed 1 June 2007.

Lycke, K., Strømsø, H.I. and Grøttum, P. (2006) 'Tracing the tutor role in problem-based learning and PBLonline', in M. Savin-Baden and K. Wilkie (eds) *Problem-based Learning Online*, 165–178. Maidenhead: McGraw Hill.

Lyotard, J.F. (1979) *The Postmodern Condition: A Report on Knowledge.* Manchester: Manchester University Press.

McAlpine, M. (2005) E-portfolios and digital identity: some issues for discussion, *E-Learning*, 2(4): 378–387.

McConnell, D. (2006) *E-Learning Groups and Communities.* Maidenhead: SRHE/ Open University Press.

McKenna, C. and McAvinia, C. (2007) 'Difference and discontinuity – making meaning though hypertexts'. Paper presented at Ideas in Cyberspace Education 3, Ross Priory, Loch Lomond, 21–23 March. Available at: www.education.ed.ac.uk/ ice3/papers. Accessed 4 April 2007.

McTaggart, A.R. and Kemmis, S. (2005) 'Participatory action research: communicative action and the public sphere', in N.K. Denzin and Y.S. Lincoln (eds) *The Sage Handbook of Qualitative Research* (3rd edition), 559–603. Thousand Oaks, California: Sage.

Major, C.H. (1999) Connecting what we know and what we do through problem-based learning, *American Association for Higher Education Bulletin*, 51(7): 7–9.

Mason, R. (1998) Models of online courses. *ALN Magazine*, 2(2): www.aln.org/alnweb/magazine/vol2_issue2/Masonfinal.htm. Accessed on 20 September 2004.

Mennin, S.P. and Martinez-Burrola, N. (1990) The cost of problem-based vs. traditional medical education, *Medical Education*, 20(30): 187–194.

Meyer, J.H.F. and Land, R. (2003) 'Threshold concepts and troublesome knowledge: linkages to ways of practising within the disciplines', in C. Rust (ed.) *Improving Students' Learning: Improving Student Learning Theory and Practice – 10 Years on.* Proceedings of the 10th Improving Student Learning Conference, 412–424. Oxford: Oxford Centre for Staff and Learning Development.

Mezirow, J. (1981) A critical theory of adult learning and education, *Adult Education*, 32(1): 3–24.

Mezirow, J. (1991) *Transformative Dimensions of Adult Learning.* San Francisco, California: Jossey-Bass.

Moore, G.A. (1999) *Crossing the Chasm* (2nd edition). Oxford: Capstone Publishing.

Murray, I. and Savin-Baden, M. (2000) Staff development in problem-based learning, *Teaching in Higher Education*, 5(1): 107–126.

Musal, B., Abacioglu, H., Dicle, O., Akalin, E., Sarioglu, S. and Esen, A. (2002) Faculty development program in Dokuz Eylul School of Medicine: in the process of curriculum change from traditional to PBL, *Medical Education Online* 7(2): www.med-ed-online.org. Accessed on 5 May 2002.

Newell, A. and Simon, H.A. (1972) *Human Problem Solving.* Englewood Cliffs, New Jersey: Prentice Hall.

Newman, J. (2004) *Videogames.* London: Routledge.

Noble, D.F. (2001) *Digital Diploma Mills: The Automation of Higher Education.* New York: Monthly Review Press.

Oliver, R. and Herrington, J. (2003) Exploring technology-mediated learning from a pedagogical perspective, *Journal of Interactive Learning Environments*, 11(2): 111–126.

O'Grady, G. and Alwis, W.A.M. (2002) 'One day, one problem: PBL at the Republic Polytechnic'. Paper presented to 4th Asia Pacific Conference in PBL, Hatyai, Thailand, December.

O'Reilly, T. (2005) What is Web 2.0?: Design Patterns and Business Models for the Next Generation of Software. Available at www.oreillynet.com/pub/a/oreilly/tim/news/2005/09/30/what-is-web-20.html?page=1. Accessed 29 October 2006.

Parlett, M. and Dearden, G. (eds) (1977) *Introduction to Illuminative Evaluation: Studies in Higher Education.* Cardiff, California: Pacific Soundings Press.

Perkins, D. (in press) 'Theories of difficulty', in N.J. Entwistle, *Student Learning and University Teaching*, *British Journal of Educational Psychology*, Monograph Series II: Psychological Aspects of Education – Current Trends. Leicester: British Psychological Society.

Perkins, D. (1999) The many faces of constructivism, *Educational Leadership*, 57(3): 6–11.

Peters, O. (1998) *Learning and Teaching in Distance Education: Pedagogical Analyses and Interpretations in an International Perspective*. London: Kogan Page.

Piaget, J. (1954) *The Construction of Reality in the Child*. New York: Basic Books.

Poikela, S., Vuoskoski, P. and Kärnä, M. (2007) 'Developing new environments for learning and knowing in problem-based education'. Paper presented at the International Problem-based Learning Symposium 2007, Re-inventing Problem-based Learning, Singapore, Republic Polytechnic. Available at www.rp.sg/symposium/downloads.htm. Accessed 2 June 2007.

Pratt, D.D. (1998) *Five Perspectives on Teaching in Adult and Higher Education*. Malabar, Florida: Krieger, Publishers.

Pratt, D.D. and Collins, J. (2006) 'Five perspectives on teaching'. Paper presented at International Problem-based Learning Symposium 2007, Re-inventing Problem-based Learning, Singapore, Republic Polytechnic. Available at www.rp.sg/symposium/download/Summary%20Paragraphs.pdf. Accessed 2 June 2007.

Ravenscroft, A. and Matheson, M.P. (2002) Developing and evaluating dialogue games for collaborative e-learning, *Journal of Computer Assisted Learning*, 18(1): 93–101.

Reagan, S., Teague, M., Atkinson, D., Jamrozik, K. and Barnard, A. (2001) 'The application of the PBL philosophy to the practical experience', Proceedings of the 3rd Asia Pacific Conference on Problem-based Learning, Little, P. *et al.* (eds), PROBLARC, Australia. the University of Newcastle, NSW.

Reeves, T. (2002) 'Storm clouds on the digital education horizon', in A. Williamson, C. Gunn, A. Young and T. Clear (eds) *Winds of Change in the Sea of Learning*. Proceedings of the 19th Annual Conference of the Australasian Society for Computers in Learning in Tertiary Education (ASCILITE), UNITEC Institute of Technology, Auckland, New Zealand, 17–26.

Rendas, A., Pinto, P.R. and Gambosa, T. (1999) A computer simulation designed for problem-based learning, *Medical Education*, 33(1): 47–54.

Rogers, E.M. (1962) *Diffusion of Innovations*. New York: The Free Press.

Ronteltap, F. (2006) 'Tools to empower problem-based learning: a principled and empirical approach to the design of problem-based learning online', in M. Savin-Baden and K. Wilkie (eds) *Problem-based Learning Online*, 174–190. Maidenhead: McGraw Hill.

Ronteltap, F. and Eurelings, A. (2002) Activity and interaction of students in an electronic learning environment for problem-based learning, *Distance Education*, 23(1): 11–22.

Salmon, G. (2000) *E-Moderating: The Key to Teaching and Learning Online*. London: Kogan Page.

Salmon, G. (2002) *E-tivities: The Key to Active Online Learning*. London: Kogan Page.

Savin-Baden, M. (2000) *Problem-based Learning in Higher Education: Untold Stories*. Buckingham: SRHE/Open University Press.

Savin-Baden, M. (2003) *Facilitating Problem-based Learning. Illuminating Perspectives*. Maidenhead: SRHE/Open University Press.

Savin-Baden, M. (2007) *Learning Spaces. Creating Opportunities for Knowledge Creation in Academic Life*. Maidenhead: SRHE/Open University Press.

Savin-Baden, M. and Gibbon, C. (2006) 'Online learning and problem-based learning: complementary or colliding approaches?', in M. Savin-Baden and K. Wilkie (eds), *Problem-based Learning Online*, 126–139. Maidenhead: McGraw Hill.

Savin-Baden and Hanney (2006) 'Project-based problem-based learning?'. Paper presented at the Association of Medial Practice conference, Leeds, January.

Savin-Baden, M. and Major, C. (2004) *Foundations of Problem-based Learning*. Maidenhead: SRHE/Open University Press.

Savin-Baden, M. and Wilkie, K. (eds) (2006) *Problem-based Learning Online*. Maidenhead: McGraw Hill.

Scardemalia, M. and Bereiter, C. (1994) Computer support for knowledge-building communities, *The Journal of the Learning Sciences*, 3(3): 256–283.

Schmidt, H.G. and Moust, J. (2000) Towards a taxonomy of problems used in problem-based learning curricula, *Journal on Excellence in College Teaching*, 11(2/3): 57–72.

Scriven, M. (1972) Pros and cons about goal-free evaluation, *Evaluation Comment*, 3(4): 1–4.

Sharpe, R., Benfield, G., Roberts, G. and Francis, R. (2006) The Undergraduate Experience of Blended E-learning: A Review of UK Literature and Practice, Higher Education Academy. Available at: www.heacademy.ac.uk/5105.htm. Accessed 5 May 2007.

Stake, R.E. (1978) The case study method in social inquiry, *Educational Researcher*, 7(2): 5–8.

Stenhouse, L. (1975) *An Introduction to Curriculum Research and Development*. London: Heinemann.

Stewart, T.M. and Galea, V.J. (2006) Approaches to training practitioners in the art and science of plant disease diagnosis, *Plant Disease*, 90(5): 539–547.

Stewart, T.M., William, R., MacIntyrea, W.R., Galea, V.J. and Steel, C.H. (2007) Enhancing problem-based learning designs with a single e-learning scaffolding tool: two case studies using Challenge FRAP, *Interactive Learning Environments*, 15(1): 77–91.

Stufflebeam, D.L. (2000) 'The CIPP model for evaluation', in D.L. Stufflebeam, G.F. Madaus and T. Kellaghan (eds), *Evaluation Models* (2nd edition), 279–317. Boston, Massachusetts: Kluwer Academic Publishers.

te Winkel, W., Rikers, R. and Schmidt. H. (2006) 'Digital support for a constructivist approach to education: the case of a problem-based psychology curriculum', in M. Savin-Baden and K. Wilkie (eds) *Problem-based Learning Online*, 159–173. Maidenhead: McGraw Hill.

Todd, S. (1997) 'Preparing tertiary teachers for problem-based learning', in D. Boud and G. Feletti (eds), *The Challenge of Problem Based Learning* (2nd edition), 130–136. London: Kogan Page.

Tosh, D., Light, T.P., Fleming, K. and Hayward, J. (2005) Engagement with electronic portfolios: challenges from the student perspective, *Canadian Journal of Learning and Technology*, 31(3): www.cjlt.ca/content/vol31.3/tosh.html. Accessed 2 June 2007.

TPLD (Team Play Learning Dynamics). Available at www.tpld.net/main.php?page= 102. Accessed 1 June 2007.

Ulmer, G. (2003a) *Internet Invention: From Literacy to Electracy*. New York: Longman.

Ulmer, G. (2003b) Web Supplement to Internet Invention. Available at www.nwe. ufl.edu/~gulmer/longman/pedagogy/. Accessed 1 May 2006.

Vygotsky, L.S. (1978) *Mind in Society: The Development of Higher Psychological Processes*. Cambridge, Massachusetts: Harvard University Press (original work published 1930).

Walton, H.J. and Mathews, M.B. (1989) Essentials of problem-based learning, *Medical Education*, 23(6): 542–558.

Wegner, S.B., Holloway, K.C. and Wegner, S.K. (1999) The effects of a computer-based instructional management system on students communication in a distance learning environment, *Educational Technology and Society*, 2(4): 145–153.

Wilkerson, L. and Hundert, E.M. (1997) 'Becoming a problem-based tutor: increasing self-awareness through faculty development', in D. Boud and G. Feletti (eds) *The Challenge of Problem-based Learning*, (2nd edition), 159–171. London: Kogan Page.

Wilkie, K. (2002) 'Actions, attitudes and attributes: developing skills for facilitating problem-based learning'. Unpublished PhD Thesis, Coventry University.

Wilkie, K. (2004) 'Becoming facilitative: shifts in lecturers' approaches to facilitating problem-based learning', in M. Savin-Baden and K. Wilkie (eds) *Challenging Research in Problem-based Learning*, 81–91. Maidenhead: SRHE/Open University Press.

Winter, R., Buck, A. and Sobiechowska, P. (1999) *Professional Experience and the Investigative Imagination*. London: Routledge.

Zimitat, C. and Miflin, B. (2003) Using assessment to induct students and staff into the PBL tutorial process, *Assessment and Evaluation in Higher Education*, 28(1): 17–32.

Index